THE PRACTICE OF COMMUNITY IN THE UNIVERSITY

Selected Speeches and Essays

James W. Wagner

Edited by Gary S. Hauk

Foreword by Jimmy Carter

Emory University
201 Dowman Drive
Atlanta, Georgia 30322
404-727-6021

ISBN: 978-1-944962-17-3

Library of Congress Control Number: 2016943289

Secant Publishing, LLC
P.O. Box 79
Salisbury, Maryland 21803

This book was designed and produced by:
Scribe, Inc.
842 South Second Street
Philadelphia, PA 19147

Editor: Gary S. Hauk
Printed in the United States of America.

Contents

Foreword

I first met Jim Wagner in 2003, when he was under consideration to be president of Emory, and I was attracted to him because he was both a fellow engineer and an idealist. He described a broad vision for the university's future that included service to the people of the world, especially within the poorest of nations. I believed he possessed the practical capability to transform that vision into reality. Once he took office, he worked to see Emory expand its influence beyond Atlanta and beyond American borders. He was especially eager to have the university engage with the Carter Center in the developing world.

I invited Jim and his wife, Debbie, to go to Africa in September 2005 with me, Rosalynn, and other Carter Center leaders. We visited some of our Center projects in health, education, economic development, and democracy in Mali, Nigeria, and Ethiopia. Jim also met with university presidents in those nations. On the flight back to Atlanta, Jim and I had what were likely some of the most significant conversations we have ever had. What he had seen of the Carter Center's work in Africa inspired long and sincere talks with me, Center staff, and his own faculty about how to move Emory toward a more active involvement in the developing world by expanding Emory's superb health programs and launching new initiatives in international service. Out of these conversations, in 2006 came the Institute for Developing Nations and the Emory Global Health Institute. These and other initiatives that followed have benefited the people of many nations and also strengthened the bonds between the Carter Center and Emory.

Jim's encouragement of Emory's involvement in global health has been recognized by substantial grants, notably from major foundations.

These particular grants recognize faculty eminence and student excellence and establish partnerships with Emory that will last for decades. Emory was an excellent institution before Jim arrived; under his leadership, it has moved to a higher level.

President Barack Obama appointed Jim as vice chair of the Presidential Commission for the Study of Bioethical Issues, indicating recognition of Jim's wise judgment and his willingness to tackle very challenging issues. Recently, when asked for three words characterizing Jim, I said, "integrity, vision, and capability."

Once every month for more than twelve years, Jim, Debbie, Rosalynn, and I have had breakfast together. For about an hour and a half, we have a relaxed conversation about what is going on at Emory and at the Carter Center and how we can bring our two institutions closer together. This informal relationship has sustained and increased the harmony and collaborative efforts of the two institutions.

I regret that Jim is stepping down as president of Emory, but I expect that he will continue to make great contributions through service of one kind or another. From my own experience, I know this is possible. We at the Carter Center will miss him. He served both Emory and the Carter Center exceptionally well.

The essays in this volume provide evidence of his leadership and his values. He committed himself to building an academic community that met and resolved the most challenging issues. I especially appreciated his support of what he calls "impossible conversations"—conversations that people typically avoid because of the discomfort they bring. I agree that a great university must be engaged in fostering and, indeed, requiring such conversations. With these and other insights, Jim provides us much to consider.

Jimmy Carter
May 1, 2016

Preface to *The Practice of Community*

The presidency—any presidency—has had the pulpit function since long before Theodore Roosevelt exulted in how bully good a platform the office is. From Lincoln's profound elocution about our better angels to FDR's "nothing to fear but fear itself," US presidents have exercised homiletic style to shape a vision for our country and chart a national way through an ambiguous present.

A university presidency provides no less bully a pulpit, although fewer modern incumbents have the rhetorical skills of their nineteenth-century forebears, who frequently came from the clergy or the humanities disciplines. In those days, custom in many liberal arts colleges—Emory College, for instance—called for the president to teach a senior-level course in moral philosophy as well as to hold forth regularly in the college chapel and, importantly, preach the baccalaureate sermon before commencement.

The modern university president similarly has ample opportunity to get out on the hustings and speak to audiences of alumni, donors, civic leaders, business executives, and conferences full of scholars. Frequently, the matter at hand is no more profound than the utility of an expanded budget for research or a bigger endowment for scholarships or a larger cadre of distinguished faculty positions. Quite often the topic of the moment is the need to maintain the university as an open pathway to careers. But sometimes the subject is the purpose of education itself. Unsurprisingly, such conversations about purpose and meaning expand to include the aims of democracy and the virtues of a fulfilling life. There is something old-fashioned about this kind of talk, something reminiscent of the nineteenth century—or a bully pulpit.

Thirteen times during his presidency of Emory University (2003–16), Jim Wagner stepped into a literal pulpit on the Emory campus to deliver the baccalaureate address to the assembled bachelor's degree candidates and their families on Mother's Day morning, the day before commencement. He found inspiration in a broad range of subjects: not only in passages from the Hebrew Bible and the Christian New Testament, but also in Robinson Crusoe, quantum physics, sailing, astrophotography, electoral politics, bioethics, the products sold by Brookstone—even the idea of the university itself.

It is this last topic that really constitutes the subject of this book—the idea that a twenty-first-century institution so variegated, ambitious, elite, and fraught with many tensions can be thought of as a community. What do the humanists have in common with the health scientists, or the undergraduates with the professional students, or the digital scholars with the archives rummagers? How does a multibillion-dollar enterprise operating with no profit margin play a role as a corporate citizen? The answers depend on the kind of vision the institution adopts for itself.

In the first months of his presidency, Jim Wagner led the Emory community in thoughtfully crafting a vision statement. As he would put it, the statement was both aspirational and confessional—a statement of what Emory wanted to be and a recognition that the university was not there yet. As the vision statement put it, Emory aimed to be "a destination university, internationally recognized as an inquiry-driven, ethically engaged, and diverse community, whose members work collaboratively for positive transformation in the world through courageous leadership in teaching, research, scholarship, health care, and social action."

This is a vision of a community whose purpose is not merely to train future contributors to the economy, but to inculcate a sense of humanity. It is a vision dependent on the practice of certain habits of mind and disciplines of being. Philosophers would call these habits and disciplines "virtues." So much the more interesting, then, to hear them being extolled by an engineer. While not exactly a convert from engineering to the liberal arts, Wagner sometimes sounds a note of earnest enthusiasm in a way that might remind Emory's Methodist founders of the fruits of a good camp meeting—hearts warmed by conviction, minds renewed by sudden insight, lives changed by reflection about the self in a universal context.

The chapters of this slim volume include selected baccalaureate addresses that Wagner delivered from the pulpit of Glenn Memorial at Emory, as well as several of his speeches on similar themes. Interspersed throughout are brief essays that appeared in *Emory Magazine*—essays that differed from the usual presidential magazine message by dwelling less on campus news and more on the ways in which a people can stay true to their vision. In short, they are about how to practice community.

Gary S. Hauk 91 PhD
Emory University

Part 1

A Place for Difficult Conversations

Address to the National Press Club
April 25, 2007

Toward a New "PC"—Passionate Civility and Practical Courage

Good morning, and thank you for joining us on this "Emory Day at the National Press Club." I must say—not only to the Emory alumni who are present but also to those of you in the Fourth Estate—that my colleagues on the faculty and in the administration who have traveled here to be part of the discussions are among the most committed, the most passionate, indeed, the most *courageous* scholars and teachers in the country. Whether their vocation is to forge a new and more deeply humane understanding of the world's religions, or to help shape health-care policy, or to expand the political franchise and democratic engagement—these are distinguished scholars whose work will repay your attention. I'm very proud to share this day with them.

Of course, all of us come to a discussion of higher education still very much affected by the events of last week in Blacksburg, Virginia. Our prayers and thoughts continue to be with the families of those who died and with the community of Virginia Tech. If we needed a reminder that the university is not an ivory tower, nothing could have demonstrated that fact more terribly, more horrifically, than those hours on the Virginia Tech campus when the university as a microcosm of our society was on display. I want to say more about this in a few minutes. But first, let me say something about our purpose for being here.

We have come here, in part, to show off this constellation of stars—just a dozen who will have to stand today for many hundreds of others. We have come here, in part, to dispel a myth or two about Emory. A university that does not play Division I basketball or football finds it hard to be noticed in our infotainment culture. Yet Emory now competes on a national and, indeed, a global stage for talent and resources. As a research university, we work at the usual things that all American universities are up to—expanding the frontiers of knowledge, slaying ignorance, discovering cures for disease, and, of course, finding places for people to park.

I want to propose, though, that while academic enrichment is a very important part of the work of a leading university, our world needs universities that can play a still more critical role. That role is one that requires courage, because the more fully we embrace it, the more profoundly we are opened to internal dissension and external criticism. That role is to provide a forum where people who disagree violently can do so without actually resorting to violence. It is a role not being played adequately by any other institution in our increasingly fractious society.

You here today don't need me to tell you what kind of world we live in. Those of you in the media report on it every day. And the rest of us—who rely on you professionals to give us fuller insight into our world—also know firsthand that American civic life has grown harsh. It's not quite the Hobbesian state of nature, where life is "solitary, poor, nasty, brutish, and short." But we may sometimes fear that we're devolving to that.

We probably can't blame it on the Internet, television, talk radio, or Dr. Spock—if anyone remembers who he was. No, most of these are, in the truest sense, mere stand-ins for ideas and movements that would find other means of expression if electronic communications did not exist. We live in a contentious world. Many who work as researchers and teachers in universities are prone to vilification, or worse, from true believers of the Left and Right—from those who oppose the use of animals to test new drugs or vaccines, no matter how many years of human life they might redeem from pain or death; from those who oppose research-driven state policies requiring the use of seat belts or the use of vaccines to prevent diseases in children; or, for that matter, from those who contest the teaching of evolutionary theory, a foundation stone of the modern life sciences. The list could go on and on in considerable detail, reminding us all of the unexpected way, at this late date in the history of the West, that science and reason themselves have become subjects of controversy. If you have former friends who now keep a distance because of political disagreement, changes in religious belief or practice, or contention over the way to raise children—well, you can count yourselves part of a growing club.

All of us are familiar with the famous line attributed to F. Scott Fitzgerald, that "the test of a first-rate intelligence is the ability to hold two opposing ideas in mind at the same time and still retain the ability to function." Less famously, Conor Cruise O'Brien described an intellectual as "someone who is prepared to admit when another has made a point in a debate." On both counts, it's fair to wonder whether our society has lost some of its capacity for instilling—or at least requiring—this kind of intellectual capaciousness, this ability to experience or understand life from another person's perspective. Can you imagine the talking heads on some of the cable TV channels and talk radio stations pausing in the middle of their heated exchanges and saying, "You know, Bill, or you know, Sean, or you know, Tim—I think you have a point there." We are a society increasingly trained to hold on like bulldogs to a narrow way of viewing things.

Here's an illustration of what I mean. Passing through an airport, I noticed in a shop a miniature glass globe, a biosphere, containing a half dozen live red shrimp and a stalk of an underwater plant. This airtight, water-filled container creates a perfect, self-contained environment: the seaweed produces oxygen for the shrimp, which in turn produce carbon-dioxide for the plant and "groom" it by eating microalgae off it. These biospheres require nothing further—no need to add water, air, food, plants, or anything else. You can put it on your desk and forget about it.

Most of us have encountered persons or communities who would like to exist in a similar kind of "bubble." Sure, they go about life in the real world of work and play, but they would prefer not to have to upset the perfectly comfortable balance of thought in their mental framework. They would prefer that no new ideas enter their self-consistent belief system and that no new mental (or moral) energy be required of them.

Such persons could be described as "fundamentalists," except that that term tends to have a particularly religious connotation for many of us these days. But fundamentalism comes in various stripes.

Consider the political fundamentalist. A study published by Emory professor of psychology Drew Westen demonstrates that after voters make up their minds about a political candidate, rational activity stops. The brain processes new information in a way that reinforces positive emotions toward a preferred candidate while tuning out information that threatens this positive response. In other words, we resist being disturbed by facts from outside our bubbles. My mind is made up—don't confuse me with the facts.

Indeed, the characteristics we normally find in religious fundamentalism—rigidity of belief, intolerance of alternative practices, and personal derogation of those who are different—some would say apply to American political life as well. A fundamentalist mind-set leads to the dangers of excluding and even demonizing those who disagree with us. I could name examples on either end of the political spectrum, but you know them as well as I do.

Universities have sometimes been accused of practicing their own form of fundamentalism. They have not always offered a welcome place for wrestling with religious faith. At some colleges and universities, faculty and students must toe a certain line defined by dogma—so that scholarship is not so much informed by faith as determined by it. At most research universities, faith is set aside as a charming anachronism, and religion is viewed through the lens of dispassionate objectivity. Both of these models ignore the capacity of human intelligence to believe one thing while passionately examining its opposite. Both also diminish the vital need for persons of differing perspectives to understand each other's intellectual constructs.

What I want to suggest is that the distinctive role of the university is to create habitats where we are safe, but where it is also impossible for us merely to exist like shrimp in a bubble. The business of a university is to set us free from our self-centered universe, to enable us to perceive the world from others' perspectives, and to empower us to make a positive impact on society. Let me repeat. The true purpose of the university is to lead us out of our self-centered universe to a place where we can gain as much insight as information, as much wisdom as knowledge.

Let me give you another for-instance. What do former president Jimmy Carter, Booker Prize–winning novelist Salman Rushdie, and the Dalai Lama have in common—besides, as you may have heard, their acceptance of faculty appointments to teach Emory students?

Earlier this year, all three were in the news because of their roles at Emory. But the other thing they share is a commitment to engaging in impossible conversations. By "impossible conversations," I mean those conversations that people tend *not* to engage in because of the discomfort caused by political differences, religious dogmatism, or the deep-seated prejudices that attach to race, gender, and sexuality. It's easier to cut off conversation than to cut through the knottiness of some issues. It's certainly easier to walk away than to walk beside someone whose views we violently oppose.

The lasting contribution of the university tradition lies in its dedication to fostering—indeed, to *requiring*—such "impossible conversations." This does not mean that we have to find resolution to every problem; but we do have to engage. Such engagement rarely happens outside of universities. It does not happen, except by accident, in the well of the US House or Senate, or in the halls of the United Nations, or in any other political venue where rhetoric is employed instrumentally, for political ends, and where the rules often are invoked to stop debate rather than enhance it. It often does not happen in our religious communities, which more frequently take the path of schism than resolution. Such impossible conversations sometimes do not even happen among married couples or in families.

Only the university is required by its mission to take pains to set the stage and define the rules for fair and honest engagement over issues of great moment. Only at a university can discussion be moderated so that all sides have an opportunity to be heard. This is why our presidential debates in America are held on university campuses—not just because the universities are willing to pay for the publicity that comes with such debates, but also because of the recognition that this is what universities do. Universities also insist that those who wish to speak leave aside hate speech and ad hominem attacks, and couch their ideas in language that assures that people will want to listen.

This all sounds nice and wonderful. Often it is messy and unpleasant. And sometimes it opens universities to public scorn. Think of the barrage of protest launched at universities in the 1980s and 1990s when they tried to establish codes by which to define civil discourse. Hate speech, carefully defined, was to be avoided; threats against persons on the basis of race, gender, ethnicity, or religion were ruled out-of-bounds. The aim was to promote the kind of community where people could trust that they could in fact articulate outrageous ideas without suggesting that their opponents should die, and could in fact be protected from such threats themselves.

Critics of both the Left and the Right came down hard on these universities, denouncing as "PC" the kind of self-definition that these communities attempted. What these critics missed was that universities are in fact engaged in a worthy kind of PC—not the "political correctness" that has been the bogeyman of so many commentators. But rather, PC as a kind of "passionate civility." Universities must have the courage to *en*courage their faculty members and students to engage passionately with the ideas that excite them and to do so civilly—with respect for the persons who espouse those ideas.

One of the prouder moments in my time at Emory occurred in February 2007, when the university community gathered in our Glenn Auditorium to talk about *Palestine: Peace Not Apartheid*, President Jimmy Carter's controversial book. Some members of the Emory community felt the need to hold one of their own community members accountable. He, in turn, wanted to explain his position more fully within the university family. The intense but civil and courteous discourse that ensued was a model for what our civilization should seek. The audience of students, faculty, and staff members—many of whom disagreed violently with Carter's perspective—did what a university (and perhaps only a university) does best: it practiced a passionate but nonviolent way of engaging respectfully, honestly, and purposefully while trying to understand complex truth.

I do not know whether anyone's opinions were changed on that day. But I do believe that some minds were changed. They were made stronger, more open, more nimble, more capable of understanding through the practice of impossible conversations.

This particular notion of courage can be deepened and extended, though. Because there's a special courage required to continue as a university "family," so-called, when the bonds of the biological family don't exist. The courageous university community adopts the practices of healthy families. The faculty members who vehemently dispute each other's arguments—as several of Emory's professors disputed President Carter's—are willing to engage passionately in the debate while remaining in community with each other. Just as Emory will not sever its ties with the Carter Center, as some have urged, neither will Carter's fiercest faculty critics sever their own ties with Emory—aggrieved as they may be. To me, this is the special quality of universities and the particular reason why we must have courage. We must give harbor to the unpopular but well-argued, the marginal but potentially fruitful—believing that in the fullness of time, some of those unlikely or unwelcome ideas, just one or two of those uncomfortable critics, may be the very ones in whom we find new meaning and hope.

Now I can hear the objections: Sure, you say—it's all well and good for tenured professors to go at each other hammer and tongs in the safety of their cloistered campuses, where nothing much is at stake and where the work of classics scholars, lab-rat feeders, and sentence diagrammers in freshman English courses has little or no impact on the lives of long-haul truckers, low-income single mothers, Wall Streeters, or our fellow human beings who suffer misery, war, and environmental degradation in places like Darfur, Afghanistan, and Nigeria. What courage is necessary when your job is guaranteed except in the event of proven malfeasance, moral turpitude, or failure to show up?

It may be that our image of the academy is still informed too much by stereotypic images of the sixties: long-haired philosophers in bell-bottoms and denim vests seeking to appear relevant to their young charges in the SDS. Let me offer another image: a middle-aged historian in a business suit lecturing to a packed hall of 250 with the Internet transmitting his every syllable to a dozen other campuses, recounting with considerable detail and passion why he has broken with a former US president, a friend and colleague of a quarter century's standing, over the critical differences in their shared devotion to the achievement of peace in the

Middle East. That, of course, would be professor of history Ken Stein, continuing the riveting "impossible conversation" that engaged so many on our campus after President Carter's publication of *Palestine: Peace Not Apartheid*. This is courage—to continue the conversation, to stay involved, to talk but also to listen, to respond.

And here is another example. For six years, Emory engaged in something we called the Transforming Community Project—an effort to engage and involve our university community, from faculty and students to administrative assistants and grounds keepers and alumni and lab technicians, in probing conversations about race in our institution. Like every other university founded in the South, and many founded in the North before the Civil War, Emory has slavery in its past. Like every other institution in America, Emory is made up of people who often have a difficult time talking frankly with each other about race, especially across racial lines. Emory was one of only several dozen colleges and universities in the country—out of more than 700 that applied—to be awarded grants by the Ford Foundation through its Difficult Dialogues program to carry out this project. In fact, we at Emory believed so much in the necessity and likely positive outcome of the project that we invested more than $2 million of our own funds in seeing it through. We wanted to transform our community, and in the process, we hoped to model the way for other American communities to be transformed. We wanted this so much that we were willing to risk failure in the attempt.

The Great Seal of the State of Georgia, which Emory of course calls home, displays the state's motto: "Wisdom, Justice, Moderation." Interestingly, these are three of the four so-called cardinal virtues on which all the rest of moral life depends. What's the fourth virtue, the one missing from the seal? Courage. It is that virtue that braces the courageous individual—or the courageous institution—to endure scorn and injury to ensure that wisdom, moderation, and justice will flourish. As you observe the progress and achievements of Emory and other research universities, we do of course want you to be cognizant of our achievements—our Nobels and Pulitzers and Rhodes scholarships, our grants and contracts, our patents and cures. But also look at us through the frame of PC—of passionate civility. *Are we passionate*—do we care? Do we care deeply and profoundly about the antagonisms and needs of our world? And do we care *civilly*—with respect for persons, with nonviolent debate at a time of violent disagreement?

If so, that is the PC test—the test that shows whether we have the *practical courage* that you have every right to expect of every university worthy of the name.

History and Wholeness

What is the consequence of deliberately or unconsciously forgetting the past? For George Santayana, famously, the consequence was being "condemned to repeat it." But for many others, such forgetting may lead to illness, brokenness, and barriers that prevent them from moving forward in life with integrity. Consider the affliction of "conversion disorder."

Occasionally, persons develop physical symptoms—say, inexplicable blindness, paralysis, or sudden inability to speak—that have no apparent physical cause. Neurological tests and other diagnoses turn up no anatomical reasons for the problem. Often, however, such afflictions are preceded by emotionally or psychologically stressful events, some trauma whose unpleasantness seems to be channeled into an actual physical disorder. Witnessing a horrific experience may lead to blindness—not because the eyes have been injured, but because the mind does not want to risk seeing more horror. Or getting angry enough to want to punch someone's lights out may feel so frightening that the mind paralyzes the arms to prevent unwanted violence.

It is not too much of a stretch to suggest that something like this can happen in institutions, even in nations, as well as in individuals: collective blindness, collective paralysis, collective inability to hear with any acuity.

Emory University, like America, has been on a long road to recovery from a kind of "conversion disorder," a kind of elective amnesia, suffered for many years by our nation as well as by Emory. The trauma to be forgotten was the inhumanity of slavery, and the resulting affliction was decades of Jim Crow laws, racism, and communal discord. In 2011, the year Emory observed its 175th anniversary, the Executive

Committee of the Emory Board of Trustees issued a statement of regret for Emory's "entwinement" with the institution of slavery during the early years of the College's life and for the harmful legacy of slavery. While the statement grew out of a campus-wide conversation prompted by our extensive, six-year Transforming Community Project, in every respect, the statement was neither a culminating end point nor exactly a beginning. It was, rather, the latest in a long series of chapters in Emory's history—some courageous, others less so—dealing with the legacies of slavery and racism.

The roots of that statement, like the roots of the university, reach deeply into America's past, and if we seek to trace out those roots, we find a particular strand gripped by Georgia clay and flourishing as early as 1836—indeed, earlier. This root we know as slavery. But we could also call it by the name of inhumanity. For it was a way of life that prevented everyone involved in it from achieving the full potential of their humanity—whether it was the enslaved, whose humanity was degraded by bondage, or the enslaver, whose humanity was eroded by hubris and blindness.

The Emory University motto, drawing on the book of Proverbs, is *Cor prudentis possidebit scientiam*, which we translate, "The wise heart seeks knowledge." In the 175th year of Emory's existence, we could be grateful that some wise hearts sought knowledge and aimed not to forget the trauma of that period, so that we could reclaim the wholeness, the integrity, of our university.

One of those wise hearts was a president, Atticus Haygood, who, in the 1880s, incurred the opprobrium of many fellow Southerners by creating opportunities for higher education for freed slaves. Another wise heart was an Emory professor, Andrew Sledd, who in 1902 risked his career in speaking out against lynching and calling his fellow Americans to the rule of law. Other wise hearts included faculty members who in the 1950s acted in behalf of desegregated public schools in Atlanta and Georgia. Still others included trustees who in 1962 took the step of suing the state for the right to integrate Emory's student body. And today, those wise hearts include men and women of all races and colors who refuse to let Emory or America forget either the trauma of the past or the long way we have come—and the long way we have yet to go—toward the full restoration of our humanity.

Our community is now recovering from its elective amnesia. It is important to the integrity and health of Emory for us to remember who we were and who we have become. Only thus can we move to a brighter future. The way the trustees put it was this: "As Emory University looks forward, it seeks the wisdom always to discern what is right and the courage to abide by its mission of using knowledge to serve humanity."

May it be so.

Address to the Twentieth Annual
Forum of National Ethics Councils
Rome, November 18, 2014

No Borders: The Importance of International Collaboration in Bioethics

It is good to speak to you today on behalf of the US Presidential Commission for the Study of Bioethical Issues—or the Presidential Bioethics Commission, for short. It has been my honor to serve as vice chair of this body since it was created by President Obama in 2009. Our commission is led by Dr. Amy Gutmann, a distinguished moral and political philosopher and the president of the University of Pennsylvania.

Dr. Gutmann and I have the privilege of working alongside nine other dedicated citizens appointed by President Obama. They are experts from wide-ranging fields, including medicine, nursing, law, science, philosophy, and ethics. I round out this multidisciplinary group: I am an engineer. Our commission is fortunate to count among its members representatives of the federal government, including a senior officer in the United States military. This roster reflects not only the diversity of the United States but also the complexity inherent in today's bioethical issues. We all know that the issues and questions that arise as medicine, science, and technology advance are complex and challenging, and they span multiple academic and professional fields.

Just as complex scientific and ethical questions do not recognize traditional academic and professional boundaries, neither do they stop at international borders. The rapid globalization of research has created not only new opportunities for collaboration but also new challenges and concerns. More than ever, we need to reach across our borders to share and receive information and wisdom. We all stand to gain from thoughtful conversations about how bioethical decision making can best be structured. And we all benefit from deepening our collective understanding of the similarities and differences in our approaches to complex scientific, biomedical, and technological issues.

I'd like to briefly touch on both the process and the substance of bioethical decision making in the United States. I begin by offering a brief history of how bioethical perspectives have been integrated into federal policy making in the United States. I'll then offer some general thoughts on how the Presidential Bioethics Commission has approached a number of challenging issues and how we are working to tackle our latest charge to consider the ethical questions raised by advances in neuroscience research. Finally, I will share some thoughts on two overarching themes that have shaped and continue to shape our commission's work: education and deliberation.

Four Decades of Commissions—and Counting

In the United States, the Presidential Bioethics Commission continues a forty-year history of panels established by the president or Congress to provide expert advice on topics related to bioethics. These groups have differed in their composition, methods, and areas of focus, but they have shared a common commitment to the careful examination and analysis of ethical considerations that underlie our nation's activities in science, medicine, and technology.

The National Commission for the Protection of Human Subjects of Biomedical and Behavioral Research is generally viewed as the first US bioethics commission. Established by Congress as part of the 1974 National Research Act, it was created soon after public revelation of the infamous Tuskegee experiments, in which the United States Public Health Service studied the natural progression of untreated syphilis under the guise of providing free health care to indigent African Americans.

The Tuskegee experiments shocked the American conscience, and consequently, the National Commission, as it is known, was charged with identifying fundamental principles for research involving human volunteers. While that commission was dissolved in 1979 after completing its work and issuing the Belmont Report, its legacy lives on because its findings were the basis for subsequent federal regulation in this area.

Since that commission's formation four decades ago, bioethics has had a steady but varied presence within the US federal government. Commissions have been established for different purposes—some to examine single issues, others to look at bioethical issues in general as they arise. As a result, there have been at least seven federal bioethics commissions over the past forty years. Unlike our European counterparts, none of the US commissions has constituted a permanent bioethics committee. Each of these groups has helped the federal government ensure that scientific research and biomedical regulation and policy proceed with awareness of and sensitivity to ethical considerations.

Most recently, each of the past three US presidents—Bill Clinton, George W. Bush, and Barack Obama—has established his own bioethics commission to explore ethical issues in science, medicine, and technology. President Obama's commission has examined synthetic biology, protections for adult and pediatric participants in research, and the ethical implications of advances in genomic and neuroscience technologies. Each of these emerging areas presents novel questions and challenges.

There are advantages and disadvantages to having standing bodies—like the United Kingdom's Nuffield Council on Bioethics—versus temporary commissions like ours. Jason Schwartz, a bioethicist and historian of medicine at Princeton University, notes that because each new US bioethics commission effectively starts "from scratch," an absence of continuity and institutional memory can pose challenges as commissions undertake their work. However, Dr. Schwartz also notes that fresh perspectives on enduring questions in bioethics can be of great value, especially in light of the rapid pace of new developments in science and medicine.

Beyond its temporary nature, another key distinction of the US government's approach to bioethical analysis is that ours is not a regulatory body. We do not make or enforce policies or laws related to bioethics. We do not provide nor do we oversee any grants or accompanying program activities. Rather, President Obama has asked that we provide him with practical, policy-oriented advice to ensure that "our nation invests in science and innovation and pursues advances in biomedical research and health care . . . in a responsible manner." We work hard to be a source of expert independent analysis and practical policy advice—recommendations that both demystify ethics and facilitate good science.

However, our special position as a presidential commission is accompanied by a directive from the president to federal agencies to help the commission. The power of this special position was critical, for example, as we sought to answer the president's question about whether current federal regulations adequately protect participants in federally supported scientific studies. The question was at the top of many minds in the wake of discovering that the US Public Health Service had conducted unethical STD research in the 1940s in Guatemala. Government officials wondered—as did we—could such unethical research happen today?

The commission quickly learned that there is no complete source of basic information—such as level of funding, number of studies, or geographic location—about the US government's current research involving human subjects. The commission therefore requested that information from the eighteen agencies that conduct most of the federal research involving human subjects. It seemed like a simple enough request—but the commission discovered that many federal departments and agencies had no ready means to provide basic information about the research they support. It took months for the commission to pull that information together.

As a result, we recommended that each department or agency that supports human subjects research should make publicly available a core set of data elements for its research programs through its own or a transagency database system, thus increasing accountability and reducing the likelihood of harm or unethical treatment of human participants in scientific research. We are already seeing change, and agencies like the Department of Defense are implementing our recommendations.

The Aim of the Present Commission

Practical policy recommendations such as these, based on sound ethical principles, are what the Bioethics Commission strives to provide. We may have been appointed by President Obama, but we are independent and have complete latitude to write our own reports and make our own recommendations. One way we demonstrate our commitment to transparency and independence is by seeking and welcoming the input of multiple stakeholders, including our global colleagues, as we go about our work.

In every one of our projects, the Bioethics Commission's approach has been characterized by an open and deliberative exchange. Our reports and recommendations, all of which have been unanimously endorsed by the commission's membership, integrate far-reaching standards, including the universal principles of beneficence, responsible stewardship, intellectual freedom, justice and fairness, respect for persons, community engagement, and democratic deliberation.

Indeed, in 2011, recognizing the increasing involvement of foreign sites and partners in human subjects research, the Bioethics Commission created an International Research Panel to advise us on the effectiveness of current federal rules and international standards for research involving human subjects. The subcommittee consisted of experts in bioethics and biomedical research hailing from ten countries: Argentina, Belgium, Brazil, China, Egypt, Guatemala, India, Russia, Uganda, and the United States. This subcommittee met on three daylong occasions—twice in the United States and once in the United Kingdom—to discuss research standards and practices around the globe. In their discussions, subcommittee members drew upon their individual expertise and decades of experience conducting research and developing policy to protect human subjects.

The subcommittee presented its findings and recommendations, which focused on biomedical research, to the Bioethics Commission. The subcommittee members agreed that over the last fifty years, the United States and many other nations have made significant progress in developing measures to protect human subjects in research. Still, the rules, standards, and practices inside and outside the United States vary greatly.

The subcommittee's proceedings and recommendations to the Bioethics Commission were posted to our website and printed in the *Federal Register*, the journal of record of the United States government. The commission took public comment on these recommendations and ultimately used both the recommendations and resulting public comments to inform its final report on human subjects protections.

In addition, the Bioethics Commission has regularly called upon experts from across the globe to present to us on the topics before us for consideration. Across the seven topics we have considered, we have heard from more than twenty experts from Canada, Australia, and various countries in the European Union.

Our current topic—the ethical issues associated with neuroscience research—is yet another area where we have been actively reaching across borders as we deliberate the issues. President Obama asked the Bioethics Commission to review the ethical considerations associated with neuroscience research and its implications as part of the BRAIN Initiative, an effort that the president is calling the next White House Grand Challenge.

The tools, technologies, applications, and implications associated with neuroscience are rapidly evolving. However, the core ethical considerations—human dignity and the essential nature of personhood—are readily identifiable, even if the specific questions raised by the technologies are not. Last December, we convened a panel with Dr. Nikolas Rose of the Human Brain Project, Jonathan Montgomery of the Nuffield Council, and Dr. Stefano Semplici of UNESCO's International Bioethics Committee to discuss international neuroscience and ethics. This panel led to a wonderful discussion about the need to coordinate and integrate fragmented research results and data, and to cultivate humility in terms of what is not yet known or understood in neuroscience.

In response to President Obama's charge, the Bioethics Commission released *Gray Matters: Integrative Approaches for Neuroscience, Ethics, and Society*. This is the first volume in our two-volume response to the president. In *Gray Matters*, the commission called for adequate and clearly demarcated funding to achieve its recommendation of integrating ethics explicitly and systematically throughout neuroscience research. This kind of integration emanates from our strongly held belief that good science is ethical science and that we cannot have one without the other.

It allows ethical insights to inform the scientific process from the very earliest moments and to consider societal implications of neuroscience research from the very beginning. Scientists should be facile in ethics, and ethicists should be facile in science.

Ethics integration—early on and throughout research—can prevent the need for corrective interventions and help build public trust in science. In short, we believe that integration prevents intervention. So much can be gained from neuroscience research, and we must ensure that such progress is not stopped because of one significant ethical failure.

As part of our report, we recommended that BRAIN Initiative-related scientific advisory bodies include substantive participation by persons with relevant expertise in the ethical and societal implications of the neuroscience under consideration.

Importantly, the commission did not recommend a single model of integration—there are many good ways to "do" ethics, and we reported on several of these. For example, one federal agency, the Defense Advanced Research Projects Agency—or DARPA—successfully combines several approaches to ethics integration, including

- consulting with an independent panel of ethics experts;
- linking project managers with ethics mentors; and
- setting aside funds for ethics consultation.

We highlight DARPA's example because we recognize that ethics recommendations can be seen as another bureaucratic obstacle in the way of scientific progress. It is clear that DARPA's integrated model has not slowed it down, nor has ethics integration drained its budget. Quite to the contrary, the integration of ethics has strengthened the design and potential impact of scientific projects.

Currently, the Bioethics Commission is actively considering the implications of neuroscience research and its applications more broadly, such as

- the ethical issues raised across stages of life—from babyhood through the golden years—and

- what neuroscience research might mean for those affected by Alzheimer's disease, Parkinson's disease, mental illness, and other neurodegenerative diseases.

As in our earlier projects, community engagement—both at home and across the world—plays a key role in our deliberations. We have held neuroscience-related sessions at eight public meetings and are on track to release our final report in early 2015. As a final step in the release of our neuroscience project for the president, we will create an educational resource: a module or primer to accompany both volumes of our neuroscience report. Like all of our reports, that education resource will also be made available to the public—for free use.

The Role of Education and Deliberation

This brings me to my last point: the central role that education and effective deliberation have played in our work. This Bioethics Commission has often noted the need for the improvement of bioethics education. Given the multidisciplinary nature of science, medicine, and biomedical research, we believe bioethics education should be available to a wide variety of disciplines at all levels.

As part of our effort to promote policies and practices that support the ethical conduct of research, innovation, and health care delivery, the commission staff, in consultation with commission members, has developed pedagogical materials for use in traditional and nontraditional educational settings. We are the first US bioethics commission to do this. We hope our successors continue this practice.

Our educational materials use the contemporary issues addressed by the Bioethics Commission to support teaching of bioethics ideas, principles, and theories across many areas of study and practice. The materials are not intended to provide a comprehensive bioethics curriculum. They do, however, complement a robust teaching strategy with contemporary examples of real-life ethical challenges addressed by a presidential commission. The materials can be used in continuing education and professional training courses, in graduate or professional school seminars, and in workplace discussion, training of institutional review boards (IRBs), and other types of settings. Education is required for informed deliberation, and deliberation enhances education at all levels.

Let me touch briefly on what deliberation means in the context of our Bioethics Commission. We believe that the best any of us can do in the face of disagreement on complex issues is to have deliberation among a wide range of experts and involved citizens in a way that is transparent to the public. Thus our commission regularly comes together to engage in open and robust dialogue—a practice that is the foundation of deliberative democracy. Democracies are better served—indeed, we are all better served as we reach across our borders—when people vigorously, thoroughly, and respectfully discuss and debate their differences. Deliberative democracy is the give-and-take of viewpoints with an aim of finding common ground. Where common ground is not possible, we believe we must work hard to achieve mutual respect.

It is not critical that we as Bioethics Commission members agree on everything, although I am proud that all our recommendations have been unanimous. What is most important is that we clearly identify issues and potential issues for our president and then reach some consensus on how to advise the navigation of those issues. It is a principle that has served our commission well within the United States and will serve us all well as we work to collaborate across borders on bioethical issues.

It is exciting to work at the intersection of science, ethics, and technology. I am grateful to join a vital tradition of offering policy-oriented bioethical advice to the United States government. I am also proud of the work of our commission and of the friendships and partnerships we have forged and continue to forge with colleagues across our nation and around the world.

We all have a lot to gain by embracing thoughtful deliberation, collaborating with one another, and fostering a mutually respectful and mutually beneficial environment for science and technology. Doing so will ensure that we are able to continue to serve humankind through the discovery, creation, and application of scientific and technical knowledge.

Part 2

The Power of the Liberal Arts in American Society

175th Anniversary Convocation Address
December 7, 2011, Glenn Memorial Auditorium

Freeing the Mind to Change the World

This morning is a rare occasion in American history, the celebration of an institution that has achieved the ripe old age of a hundred and seventy-five. Not many colleges or universities in the United States are older—fewer than a hundred, in fact. When you consider that some four thousand institutions of higher education exist in the United States today, longevity certainly stands out as one of Emory's distinguishing characteristics.

But we would be using our time this morning unwisely if all we wanted to celebrate was endurance and the survival of an institution through the vicissitudes of the last two centuries. So let's use this occasion to get to the heart of the matter, to learn what we can about an institution's soul. The truth is that there is a kind of tension discernible there. It can be seen in Emory's history, a tension that also pervades our present and is likely to shape our future.

Now tension is not necessarily a bad thing. In fact, it is essential to progress. The progress of a barge up a river depends on the right amount of tension in the cable that links it to the tugboat ahead. Drag and the massive inertia of the barge's cargo resist progress. The work of the tugboat's crew and the tug's mighty engines impart momentum. But with too little tension, there is no progress; and with too abrupt an acceleration, the cable will snap and progress will be lost. Genuine progress comes in the necessary tension between change and continuity—or, let's say, between aspirations and the status quo.

There is also another tension in Emory, as in every other university, simply because it is a very human organization. On one hand, Emory has claimed for itself an intention to live by exalted and noble ideals and the highest of aspirations, believing that education is one of the most powerful forces for good in the world. On the other hand, those of us who live and work here and who believe deeply in those ideals and aspirations are also daily aware of the limits of our capacity to achieve them. So Emory will never be perfect. Its progress will never be complete. We can say with pride that Emory is a quite different institution than the one that opened its doors in the 1830s, just as America is in many ways a quite different country than the one in which Emory was founded. But we are still in many respects a lot like our forebears, and the tension with which we live, between our aspirations and the status quo, is in many respects a lot like theirs.

Let me give an illustration. Looking through Henry Bullock's history of Emory, published in 1936, you come across some old-sounding language used by the founders to describe why they were starting a college a hundred years earlier. It is easy to be distracted by their quaint diction and possibly antiquated notions. Our Emory founders were not what we would think of as modern educators. Here, for instance, is Ignatius Few, Emory's founding president, reflecting on the aims of the college shortly after the end of its first semester, in 1838:

> [Emory's] pupils will . . . receive the doctrines of [Christian] revelation with the simplicity of little children, [but] they will [also] learn that the most recondite science, and the most perfect polish of . . . the human mind . . . are compatible with the humility and . . . faith of the disciples. . . . The intellectual Titan . . . who shall wield the armor . . . of science, will war not *with* but *for* heaven.

This may sound to us like the beginning of a Sunday school lesson, with its references to revelation and discipleship and heaven. But it is actually a somewhat bold declaration for a community in which education had barely gained a toehold and where piety outweighed book learning. Recall that in Georgia in the 1830s, agriculture was the dominant economy, and illiteracy was twenty times higher in Georgia than in Massachusetts. Even towns as large as Macon lacked a single schoolteacher. And even though the University of Georgia was formally incorporated in 1785, it took another sixteen years before the first students enrolled at Athens. So education was not exactly a high-profile enterprise or a priority when fifteen students began classes in Oxford, two years after Emory received its charter.

Yet here is President Few, calling for intellectual titans who will gird themselves with the armor of science as well as the virtues of faith. In the words of Charles Wesley, it's a vision to unite knowledge and piety. It is really a daring call, a summons to add the power of intellect to the driving force of faith, to bring the same rigor and discipline to bear on the mind that Methodists for decades had applied to their hearts. For many of those Methodists, and for others of that society in that day, the liberating potential of education and the refinement of intellect posed a threat to Christian belief and to the status quo. And here is President Few saying it's okay—our people need what a liberal education can give to its young men: a broader understanding, a deeper wisdom, a more agile judgment. These things will strengthen and free them as individuals and thereby, potentially, strengthen and free us all.

Of course, we must not lose sight of the frail humanity of the founders either. We at Emory began this anniversary year with a statement of regret by the trustees for Emory's entwinement with the institution of slavery during the college's early years. The access to strength and freedom available through a liberal education was limited at Emory to white males. For young women, the Methodists in 1836 established a separate college in Macon—Wesleyan College—and for African Americans, it would be another three decades before formal education would even be possible in Georgia.

So what we find in retrospect is that Emory's founders embodied the tension inherent in the human condition. On the one hand, they could see the good and aspire to it; on the other hand, their entanglement in the complex bonds of history, society, and human folly created a drag on motion toward the very good that they envisioned. That predicament is what the great theologian Reinhold Niebuhr referred to when he said that our humanity makes us capable of conceiving of our own perfection, but it also makes us incapable of achieving it. *The human spirit makes us capable of conceiving of our own perfection but incapable of achieving it.*

Our forebears could conceive of a kind of education that would produce builders and leaders of a better society, yet that better society was always somewhere over the horizon. If we are truthful, we know that we have inherited their legacy fully, for we also find ourselves as individuals, as a university, and as a society, in the same predicament. We believe that education empowers people, yet we struggle as a society to make it more available. We know that research has led to better lives for millions, yet we debate whether public resources should be used for research that could (not tomorrow, but sometime down the road) enlarge the public good. We see the need for more physicians and other health care professionals but are caught in a budget bind that threatens support for educating them. In so many ways, we embrace the nobility of our historic aspirations while sensing that the fulfillment of those aspirations is always around the corner from tomorrow.

One of the glories of the kind of liberal education that Emory has tried to foster for the past 175 years is that it opens our eyes to this predicament, reframes it as an exciting challenge, and gives us the skills to try to move beyond it. Study in the humanities awakens our appreciation of the human comedy as well as human tragedy. Study in the arts nurtures our own inclination, however feeble, to give expression to our deepest longings and hopes and aspirations. Study in the sciences encourages discovery and experimentation that insists on testing hypotheses, examining possibilities, and conducting the necessary trial and error that lead to knowledge and progress.

If we need any justification for this kind of liberal education, this kind of freeing of the mind, all we need to do is recall the Emory men and women who have manifested the virtues of a liberal education through their achievements—men and women who have exercised keen analysis, critical thinking, moral judgment, and the capacity to transform life through the power of minds and hearts fully engaged. They also inspire us to acquire, like them, a working set of virtues. And they teach us that the deep commitment to these virtues over time helps one to form an authentic character and to pursue a calling with integrity.

Think of them. Think, for instance, of C. Vann Woodward, who grew up in a tiny town in Arkansas in the 1910s and '20s, but was shaped intellectually by a book-loving mother, a teacher father who had graduated from Emory College, and a beloved uncle who also had graduated from Emory and became the college's dean. Vann Woodward would grow up to become one of the great and influential American historians of the twentieth century, despite the fact that he found his history courses at Emory College dull and the books he read in graduate school poorly written and full of implausible premises. By questioning the received history of the South, by examining that history with a fresh perspective, and by exercising a prose style that made history bracing rather than boring, he broadened our understanding of not just this region but America, and not just America but humanity. His aspirations overturned the status quo.

Or think of James Dombrowski, John Griffin, and Jamie Mackey—three white men from three different states in the Deep South, who graduated from Emory College in three consecutive decades between World War I and World War II, when the Jim Crow system of apartheid appeared to be a firmly settled way of life in the American South. One was a minister and an artist; one was a sociologist and an educator; one was a lawyer and a conservationist as well as a politician. In different ways, they exhibited the remarkable aspiration and capacity of human beings to grow beyond the conventions in which they have been raised. They also worked in their separate arenas to undermine a pernicious status quo by creating opportunities in education, public service, and community building for anyone who felt the call to follow those paths, regardless of race.

Or think of Henry Bowden, Emory College and Law graduate, who in 1961 said to a group of alumni, "Emory should want no part of the status quo." Unwilling to abide by the status quo of a segregated South that would doom his alma mater to remaining a second-tier university, he helped guide Emory and the state of Georgia out of the path that would have led to a segregated mediocrity and onto a path leading to an excellence that reflected the full scope of human potential.

Or think of Eléonore Raoul and Lettie Pate Whitehead Evans and Evangeline Papageorge and others, who, without fanfare or fuss but with great effectiveness, paved the way for generations of women to succeed at Emory and beyond. We might note in passing the degree of cleverness honed in Eléonore Raoul by the liberal arts tradition at the University of Chicago. It was there that she found the aspiration, imagination, and temerity to seize the day in 1917 by enrolling in the Emory School of Law while the chancellor who opposed coeducation was out of town. What a way to move beyond the status quo!

Or think of Asa Yancey, the first African American doctor to become an attending physician at Grady Hospital, which had been built in the form of an H to separate the care for whites from the care for blacks. Can we exercise our own imaginations and draw on our own human experience to reflect on what that pioneering work must have been like for Dr. Yancey in the late 1950s and early 1960s? We honor that aspiration that helped to upend and reshape the status quo.

We celebrate these men and women, these makers of history, because they have incarnated, have brought to manifest reality in their own flesh-and-blood lives, the qualities that we hope to impart, or to strengthen, by education in a liberal arts university. We celebrate them because they have imbued their own spirits into this university, giving back what they received, and strengthening the institution's character and resolve to be a force for positive transformation in the world through the power of education, research, and service. As a university community, we take from them the determination to follow the light of learning down whatever path it illumines, the courage to speak a hard-won truth as we see our way along that path, and the hope and faith that in the end, our path will lead to a brighter horizon for those who come after us on this journey.

In closing, it's those who come after us that I would like us to think about. Looking forward to the next twenty-five years, it's fair to ask how posterity will judge our own faithfulness in living out the virtues of a liberal education. Will those who follow us see aspirations that challenged the status quo and, through the tension of that challenge, led to progress? Will they be able to thank us for exercising keenness of thought, breadth of imagination, and capacity for moral judgment? Will they see an effort to transform life through minds and hearts fully engaged?

Despite the realism of Reinhold Niebuhr's observation about human imperfection, we can be grateful for what we have seen of

Emory's past, and we can be encouraged by what we know of some of our current colleagues and community members.

Just last month, for instance, the renowned German theologian Jurgen Moltmann, a former Woodruff Visiting Professor in the Candler School of Theology, joined in conferring the certificate of theological studies on nine women at the Lee Arrendale State Prison northeast of Atlanta. This program grew out of the work of Candler alumna Susan Bishop and Candler ethics professor Elizabeth Bounds in ministering to women in prison. As one observer noted, the program's emphasis on critical thinking skills helps students see their own experiences in broader theological and social contexts—and thereby gives them the foundation for transformation. This sounds like a kind of challenge to the status quo.

Our faculty also continue to experiment with adapting the traditional liberal arts curriculum in order to meet the needs of our society for critical thinkers, perceptive analysts, and effective communicators—for men and women who can bring creative and nimble minds to address our most pressing issues with integrity and courage. The Piedmont Project, now ten years old, has taught faculty members who are themselves superb teachers how to weave the topic of sustainability into their courses. These faculty members are awakening and sharpening students' capacities in a world whose resources are growing more constrained. This sounds like a challenge to the status quo.

Similarly, the James Weldon Johnson Institute for the Study of Race and Difference, founded by our late faculty colleague Professor Rudolph Byrd, continues the hard work of facilitating honest—even risky—conversation about race. This is one way to take steps toward a more just society. The vision statement of the institute serves as an apt summary of what the liberal arts themselves aim to achieve: "The vision of the Johnson Institute is an open but applied mind committed to the creation of new scholarship and social advocacy serving all of humankind." This sounds like a challenge to the status quo.

Or think of the work being done by our health sciences researchers to improve the lives of millions around the world through new preventives, diagnostics, and therapies—for example, the work of Don Stein in treating traumatic brain injury with progesterone, or the work of Lynn Sibley in transforming the way whole communities in Ethiopia practice maternal and newborn health care.

We should be heartened by these examples. While we cannot and should not ignore the great and grave disruptions that our society is now experiencing, we can celebrate that the liberal arts still have the power to educate people who work for positive transformation in the world to change the status quo.

As we turn a page and begin a new quarter century that will take us to our bicentennial, let us take heart from the examples of those history makers whom we honor today; let us renew our determination to see clearly the circumstances in which we find ourselves; and let us draw ever more completely on the powers bequeathed to us in the Emory legacy of the liberal arts. In doing so, let us remain committed to the fundamental elements of the original vision of Ignatius Few, reinforced by leaders throughout the decades, to provide an education of the heart and mind; to perceive and answer the call to faith, hope, and compassion; to be empowered by the noble discipline of the intellect; and to strive to be increasingly a university known for courageous leadership. While we know that perfection lies always out of reach, the responsible stewardship of our legacy lies in our striving.

Enabling and Ennobling

Some twenty or more years ago, in the early 1990s, Emory had no formal mission statement, but we were required by our accrediting agency to develop one. So Emory's first Provost, Dr. Billy Frye, drafted one, and it contained a memorable line. It said that Emory believes "education is the most powerful social force of our time for enabling and ennobling the individual, and that the privilege of education entails an obligation to use knowledge for the common good." I love that phrase "enabling and ennobling."

We are familiar with the notion of enabling—enabling someone for a career or for graduate or professional school, and so on. It may be the primary reason that you put Emory on your list of prospective colleges. You expected to gain knowledge, skills, and maybe even some Emory "brand value" so that you would be better enabled for success. Enablement is the component of your education that statisticians claim makes college worthwhile—Americans with college degrees suffer unemployment at half the rate of the overall population; they can expect lifetime earnings of $1 million more than what they would have made with a high school degree alone. By such measures, universities in general, and Emory in particular, have been very enabling.

On the other hand, the other half of Dr. Frye's phrase—that word "ennobling": that may be a less-obvious gift that you will take with you from this place. But being at Emory has in fact given you nobility, and you have given nobility in return. I want to suggest how that has happened, and then I want to challenge you to keep up the practice of ennobling for the rest of your lives.

When faculty and administrators measure the degree to which we have enabled you as students, we use records of achievement and methods of assessment—grades and scores and performance rankings. Those are perfectly appropriate and necessary in classrooms, businesses, and athletic competitions. There is nothing wrong with meritocracy based on these measurements. In fact, meritocracy is important; it helps us determine, for instance, who merits admission to Emory, though I wish that Emory had room and resources to enroll all who merit admission.

But if enabling is understood as enhancing the capacities of people in a way that allows us to measure merit, ennobling is something quite different. It is a way of lifting persons up, elevating them, and recognizing their value *for reasons other than merit.*

We can gain some insight into this understanding through one of the parables of Jesus. It is a story about a landowner who goes into town one day to hire day laborers to work in his vineyard. He comes early in the morning and offers a day's wage, and soon enough, some workers are off to his vineyard to work. Needing more workers, the landowner returns to town again at 9 a.m., noon, 3 p.m., and 5 p.m., each time recruiting additional workers. The story makes no mention of his negotiating a wage with any but the first workers he recruited. At the end of the day, the landowner comes to settle up and chooses to pay every single worker the same amount, a full day's wage—much to the alarm of those who arrived first. And why not? What the landowner did seems unfair. The tired workers who had been there all day received no more than those who had arrived after the heat of the day to work only a short time. All were treated equally. How "antimeritocratic" can you get!

But the point of the parable is not to undervalue merit. Instead, the story asks us to think beyond merit—to recognize that people have value beyond what they can achieve and earn. Sure, you will be a success if you apply the abilities that you have. But you are more valuable than that, just as those around us are more valuable than the sum of their achievements and what they can do for us. This is not such a foreign idea. After all, we value newborns and the most elderly among us for reasons other than their current abilities or utility. This conferring of value on persons without regard to their ability is ennobling.

At Emory you have experienced and practiced ennobling. Recall the first days of your freshman year. For many, if not most of you, some of your deepest friendships were made during those first days and weeks on campus—friendships destined to last a lifetime. In fact, just a week ago, while leaving my office, I encountered seven of you who had arranged for a photographer and had purchased engraved bracelets to commemorate the friendships formed in your freshman year. Those friendships have lasted through commencement and, you hope, will endure forever.

What happened during the early days of your freshman year? I would suggest that you experienced the phenomenon I'll call "freshman ennoblement." Being thrown into a strange new living arrangement where expectations of you were high, established friendships were few, and waves of homesickness threatened to crash, you had little preestablished reputation by which people could judge and esteem you. Something led you and your classmates to think about yourselves and others differently. In those humbling and possibly frightening circumstances, you were more likely to encounter each person as a potential friend, regardless of merit. Your a priori assumption was that the other would be worthy of friendship. You ennobled them in that way and hoped that they in turn might ennoble you by a reciprocal act of friendship. With no knowledge of the merits of past accomplishments, you gave and received ennoblement by the expression of being worthy of friendship. You lifted other persons up—and were yourselves lifted up—to a place of nobility.

Nobility does not function by merit. It is not something we can earn for ourselves. We can gain respect through our own efforts, we can even become feared or envied, but we cannot seize nobility or assign it to ourselves. It has to be given to us by others. The best way to hope to attain it is to be an example of giving it, to contribute to a community ethos in which the ennoblement of others is the norm.

During the week of spring break, I traveled to East Asia—to Seoul, Beijing, Nanjing, and Shanghai—visiting at four universities, five alumni events, two government agencies, and one NGO. We raised a little money, formed some relationships, and learned from our alumni. A couple of the alumni events were attended by students who will be freshmen here in just a few months. I spoke briefly about the value of being fully educated in Emory's liberal arts tradition and the importance of the humanities as an underpinning for professional and nonprofessional pursuits. And then, during the Q&A that followed, a young woman asked me what I thought it meant to be human.

Not having been asked that question before, I hadn't formed a ready answer. But I found myself saying that beyond biological and anthropological definitions, being human is a status that we bestow on each other. To be more than merely biologically human requires some relationship with other human beings individually and in community. If that is true, then we have the option to ennoble others with humanity, and we ourselves are fully human only as a gift from others.

This is the point of another parable that has a place in many religions, from Judaism to Hinduism, Buddhism, and Christianity. It's the story about the difference between hell and heaven. In both places, people are seated at a banquet table with their hands bound to impossibly long utensils—a fork and a spoon fully four feet long. While the people can reach the food with these utensils, they cannot possibly turn the long utensils around to feed themselves. In hell, the banqueters are tortured by hunger in the presence of abundance. In heaven, though, the banqueters realize that everyone can eat if they feed each other by reaching their utensils across the table. In this story, food, like ennoblement and like humanity, can be given only by others.

Just so, you have fed others and have been fed by others, ennobling them and being ennobled in turn, not just through your freshman friendships, but

- when you cheered Emory for accepting the challenge to care for the first two patients ever treated in the Western hemisphere for Ebola virus disease;
- when you did something so simple as listening respectfully and waited to reply while someone else made an argument you disagreed with;
- when you volunteered to serve those who are not enabled;
- when you contributed to or administered a hardship fund;
- when you reacted with collective indignation and warm support in behalf of those who suffer racism and injustice, from the overt and intentional to the subtle or ignorant; and

- when you have forgiven those who repent of unmeritorious action, restoring their nobility.

You have done all of this in the understanding that when anyone is threatened or diminished, all risk being diminished, and none are ennobled. And when others are lifted up—just like the diners with the long spoons, just like all of those called to the vineyard by the master—all have the potential to be lifted up.

I conclude with this thought. Those like us, who are enabled and privileged with intellect and opportunity, have an ethical responsibility to work intentionally to lift others to nobility. Caring deliberately about people as people—whether they are imperfect, incomplete, different, or opposed to us—is the only way to counter a culture of cynicism and movements that confuse uniformity with unity.

What do I mean? We must be critical thinkers concerning *ideas*, but we can avoid being critics of *people*. All of us to some extent fear the opportunity to take risks, to be creative and expressive, because our culture encourages us to fear criticism. Ideas should do battle, not people.

On a global scale, failure to ennoble others has resulted in political entities, even terrorist entities, that envision the possibility of peace only in a world where all must be the same—one culture, one religion, one government, one state. But there can never be peace if we are unable to see the unique nobility of others.

This lesson easily can be lost unless we think about it deliberately—even when it is unfashionable to do so. Let us strive to practice this ability to give and receive the gift of nobility. Ennobling others is not a requirement for you to succeed in competition or business. But as the master of the vineyard asserts, achievement alone is insufficient to gauge the value of a person, and ennobling others as you are able is essential in order for you truly to *feel* successful—to enjoy fully whatever gain the rest of the world associates with success.

So my prayer for you is that you will take from Emory your heightened abilities and nobility, using them to continue experiencing the deep satisfaction and joy of lifting others.

Published in the *Atlanta Journal and Constitution*, Op-ed Page
December 30, 2004

What the World Needs Now Is . . . Thought

Recently, a well-educated, bright, and articulate woman with a successful professional career posed to me this question: What is the practical value of the liberal arts these days, especially at the prices colleges charge? In other words, how do you, as a university president–and one with an engineering background–justify schooling that does not necessarily put students on a clear path to wealth?

These questions assume that the purpose of an education is to make money, and that liberal arts graduates don't make much. Neither assumption is well founded.

Regarding the second, my colleagues in the philosophy department might point out that philosophy majors are highly sought by law schools and medical schools. The English department might recall a recent *New York Times* report that US companies spend more than $3 billion annually to teach their employees how to write: certainly job assurance for English majors.

Colleagues in Emory's School of Medicine and Goizueta Business School might note that their professions value mental nimbleness and the capacity for effective human interaction at least as much as ingrained (maybe inflexible) training. They value quality of mind as well as specific skills.

Of course, engineers, medical professionals, and technical experts continue to learn as they make progress against disease, hunger, and the barriers of time and space. But however much our technology might be an aid to civilization, it is not the thing itself. Our culture was developed by minds driven to know what is other, what is different. That kind of knowing comes from the liberal arts.

And that takes us back to that first assumption, about the purpose of education.

When we look at what happened on September 11, 2001, we see the most technologically advanced nation in history humbled not by technology but by human inventiveness at the service of ideology. In the days following that terrible event, the most pressing question was not about our technology but about "why they hate us." At Emory, we found that suddenly our experts in Islam, Arabic, and Middle Eastern history and culture were in great demand. We gave thanks that Emory and other universities offered an intellectual home for scholars in history, religion, literature, philosophy, and other liberal arts for the sake of our civilization.

Higher education should make it possible for men and women to lead better lives. But a better life includes not only—and maybe not even especially—greater employability and material comfort. A better life is one freed *from* ignorance and freed *into* the life of the mind to do the work of the world. The true purpose of higher education is to lead us out of our self-centered universe to a place where we can perceive the world from other perspectives and bring understanding and moral imagination to bear on our communities. Higher education is as much about gaining insight as it is about gaining information; as much about seeking wisdom as it is about seeking knowledge.

Viewed in this light, the life of the mind will always be essential to our civilization. Our personal experiences and "data base" are incomplete until we deeply understand the history, religion, sociology, and literatures of others. By strengthening understanding among us, the life of the mind weakens the forces that pull us apart.

The arts and humanities do not simply entertain us through story, image, music, and dance. They open us up to the mind, heart, and soul of each other. This freedom is worth a high price indeed.

Delivered at the University of Delaware
October 5, 2011

Inquiry-Driven Engineering: One of the Liberal Arts

From their ancient roots through their medieval history, universities came to define liberal learning as the means for students to identify and refine their most natural learning style and then, having experienced the thrill of learning, to fuel a life of the mind, to enjoy for a lifetime the pursuit to satisfy an insatiable desire for knowledge. Engineering was not welcomed into the academic community until late in the modern period, and that welcome is still incomplete. When we engineers focus too narrowly on the professional nature of our discipline, we often exclude thought and discussion about why we live, not merely how we live. Understanding inquiry-based engineering as a "liberal art" opens possibilities for engineering to be counted among the essential ways of thinking for those who would consider themselves fully educated in the future.

It is an honor to be invited to return to my alma mater to share a few thoughts about the discipline of engineering and the future of engineering education.

It has been observed before that the only constant is change. Constant change was evident even in my time as a student here. It has been amusing to reminisce about some of the transitions that took place in what was then the Department of Electrical Engineering during the early 1970s. We were expected to arrive on campus in the fall of 1971 having mastered the use of one of two approved models of slide rules, with which we were expected to do simple multiplication and division as well as trigonometric, exponential, and logarithmic calculations. It was not until our senior year that those who could afford them were permitted to use electronic calculators in certain approved classes. We arrived freshman year, slide rules in hand, to encounter the equations to calculate the criticality of an enriched uranium fission reactor of the sort that was actually housed in DuPont Hall at the time. That same course taught the fundamentals of Fortran IV programming using decks of punch cards to be processed by the university's single mainframe computer. Again, by our senior year, we and the world had gravitated to remote data entry through hardwired keyboards stationed around campus.

By the time I graduated in four years, resistor-transistor logic and diode-transistor logic had been replaced by transistor-transistor logic, with logic gates and flip-flops operating at speeds up to 40 MHz. In the classrooms and laboratories, analog systems still were king, and asynchronous logic held its own with the synchronous world. There was even a smattering of philosophy and ethics. Fourier theory was understood to be an alternative way to view a world of time-domain signals. To study stability criteria, we were assigned problems like this: If animal A eats animal B, and animal B eats grass, and the land produces so many pounds of grass per acre, what are the singularities in the solutions to the developed differential equations that indicate the average stable carrying capacity? It was a question about the environment!

We had professors who had worked in secret labs developing noise-reduction theories and systems to improve radar technology. Professor Robinson wrote a paper titled, "If Newton and Leibnitz Were Alive Today," hypothesizing that developments in digital computation were so powerful that there would be no need to pursue analytical solutions to differential equations.

But with all of that change and our continuing eagerness for newness, for the next great thing, we sometimes overlooked the potential to deliver more-lasting educational objectives that only universities can deliver. My topic today asks us to focus on one such deliverable—that our engineering students might also be liberal learners.

You might suspect that in choosing this topic—building a case that the engineering disciplines can be counted among the liberal arts—I may simply be trying to rationalize how an engineer like me could claim any right to serve a liberal arts university like Emory, a university that lacks an engineering program altogether. But my purpose is really to offer a broader perspective on our discipline and its ramifications for how we teach it, and how we engage with society.

The power of the discipline of engineering thought needs to be better appreciated not just for its agility in problem solving but also for its ability to prepare the mind for three human essentials—broad-minded citizenship, appreciation of beauty, and achievement and integrity of one's identity. In accomplishing those things, engineering can and should claim to be shaping the intellect and the character of its practitioners every bit as well as the more traditional liberal arts curricula that have been around for millennia. But the degree to which engineering education and practice can instill these capacities will depend on attention to pedagogical practices.

For too long, we engineers have accepted and enjoyed the description given to us as "problem solvers." The implication is that when someone else envisions a technological goal or encounters or stumbles upon a problem, especially one with a technological solution, the project can be assigned with great confidence to the engineer. But to imagine that the role of the university is to educate problem-ready engineers who are merely waiting for society to dream the dreams or confront the issues of the day is to imagine too little of our universities and the engineers that we educate. An engineer driven by inquiry rather than mere utility understands the opportunity and responsibility not merely to solve problems defined by others, but to be engaged in society, to become the dreamer, the problem definer, and then ultimately the problem solver.

Historical Resistance to Engineering in the University

Old assumptions die hard. Ironically, we engineers may be the ones providing life support for these outdated assumptions. Engineering education has long been understood, incorrectly, to be inadequate preparation of the mind fully to enjoy and contribute to the human experience in the same way as those minds that benefit from a traditional liberal arts education. History certainly confirms this bias.

From ancient and medieval times through the late 1800s, there were only two kinds of engineering—military and civilian (or civil). Entrée into those professions did not require academic certification. Instead, to become a military engineer, one volunteered or was conscripted into military service. Civilian engineers, on the other hand, entered the profession through the guild and apprentice systems, working in a hands-on setting with those who had skills and experiences to pass on. As a result, there was little interest in expecting that engineers might be candidates for education in the formal academic system of universities where the liberal arts reigned.

C. H. Cramer chronicles some of this history of academic engineering in the introduction to his 1980 history of the Case Institute of Technology, now Case Western Reserve University. He tells the story of the breakthrough of the engineering and applied sciences disciplines into the academy, introducing what had been called the mechanics arts into the halls that had housed, for so many years, only the liberal arts.

Initially, the French were the most progressive adopters of engineering education for civilians. In 1747, they established the first of many *Écoles Nationales*, with the first one focused on bridges and highways. Soon, the Germans and the Russians followed suit. And for nearly a full century, these continental European institutes were alone in their pursuits. During the same period, the British pursued and perpetuated the classical liberal arts education. They agreed with Plato that the mechanics arts were unsuitable occupations for an educated citizenry.

In America, the first colleges and universities were established on the models of Oxford and Cambridge and thus became similarly bound to a classical definition of university education—to prepare a literate clergy, educated gentlemen, and a necessary supply of lawyers and doctors. Only in the United States Military Academy at West Point, established in 1802, was engineering taught—military engineering, of course. Nevertheless, engineers were in high demand for design and construction of harbors, roads, and soon, railroads. Civilian demands for engineering talent quickly outstripped supply, and military engineers began to resign their commissions early in order to take more lucrative civilian employment. Still, American universities resisted the demand to educate engineers and scientists.

Jeremiah Day, president of Yale for twenty-three years, defended the classical approach to university education in a report of 1828: "The young merchant must be trained in the accounting room, the mechanic in the workshop, and the farmer in the field." Science might be taught for "the discipline and the furniture of the mind," but it was not acceptable to aspire to become a practitioner of science, a physicist, or an engineer. He even commented on how troubling it was to contemplate teaching such subjects, noting that "those whose researches have carried them so far beyond these simpler truths . . . come back to them with reluctance and distaste."

Even when Yale, in 1847, opened what later became the Sheffield Scientific School, its students were not permitted to sit in chapel with regular academic students. At Dartmouth, students studying science and modern languages attended classes in the wintertime, when the students of more "noble" disciplines were off campus making money as tutors.

The pattern began to change through partnership between wealthy corporate leaders and progressive educators. Thus Stephen van Rensselaer saw to the birth of Rensselaer Polytechnic Institute in 1824—the first such institution in the English-speaking world. Similarly, Yale and Harvard began programs, but apparently only halfheartedly. The first graduate of Harvard's program did not emerge until nine years after it began. Indeed, Cramer reports that prior to the Civil War, only six institutions of applied science existed in the United States, producing only three hundred graduates.

Even after the doors of the academy grudgingly opened to our ilk, use of the words "science" and "scientific" was avoided. Scientific equipment was referred to as philosophical apparatus, scientific laboratories as philosophical chambers. The bachelor of arts degree was king. Heaven forbid that there should be offered a bachelor of science degree, and so bachelor of philosophy degrees were offered by some institutions instead. (The doctor of philosophy degree is still the terminal degree given by most universities in disciplines of science and engineering.)

The Lincoln administration and the Civil War brought recognition of the need for education in science and engineering. The 1862

Morrill Act, establishing land-grant universities, provided federal funds to support the study of agricultural and mechanical arts at universities. During this same period, a cluster of technology-focused institutions was established: Boston Tech (later MIT) in 1861; the School of Mines at Columbia in 1864; Cornell and Lehigh Universities in 1865; the Stevens Institute in 1870. Here at Delaware, civil engineering was part of the science curriculum in 1850, but degree programs in engineering were not established until 1891.

Although the doors were open, attitudes were slow to change. The disdain for science and engineering within the academy is illustrated in a story told about a promising classics major at Oberlin College in Ohio in the 1880s. The student's name was Robert Millikan. Yes, this is the fellow that would go on in the early twentieth century to win a Nobel Prize in physics for a body of work that included establishing the coulombic charge of an electron. The story goes that Millikan's Greek professor approached him to teach an introductory physics course. When Millikan protested that he was not prepared to do so, his professor stated confidently, "Anyone who can do well in my Greek can teach physics." In this case, it turned out that the professor was right, but his disdain for the sciences and engineering was typical.

Eventually, the role of universities in pursuing science and engineering education and research accelerated. Vannevar Bush's report in 1945, *Science–The Endless Frontier*, convinced the Truman administration that the US science and technology agenda should be pursued through our universities rather than through national laboratories or science cities. This was to be a policy unlike those in other developed nations and led to the birth of the National Science Foundation, the National Institutes of Health, defense research funding offices, and thus the burgeoning of the American research university.

The Purposes of the Liberal Arts

Now that the mechanics arts of engineering are not only admitted into but expected to function in what was traditionally the exclusive realm of the liberal arts, it's fair to ask: Do we merely coexist with the liberal arts, or do we bring something to them? To begin to answer that question, consider just what we mean by the liberal arts and how engineering might overlap with them.

Recall first what liberal learning is all about. It has nothing to do with political persuasion or cultural attitudes. It is not "liberal" education as opposed to "conservative" education. Ancient accounts go back to Cicero's time in the first century BCE. It was a time when the citizenry, especially the aristocracy, the freed persons, could cultivate a life of the mind—when attention to matters of survival could, for some, take a back seat to matters cerebral. And so there arose education *liberalis*—education suitable for free persons, those liberated both politically from subservience and, to a degree, economically from subsistence. From the education of the liberated came liberal education. It was necessary in those times that slaves and servants should be trained in the so-called "servile arts" and that those employed in the trades would be educated in the "mechanics arts." But the free citizen was expected to pursue an education beyond training—education in the liberal arts.

Liberal education had, and still has, only two primary purposes. First, liberal education is intended as a means for the student to identify and hone a personal learning style. We as engineers tend, most often, to be linear and logical thinkers. Humanists tend more often to follow more parallel or branching paths to form opinions and express thoughts.

Once students develop an understanding and command of their own learning style, they are still only half educated, because the second purpose of liberal learning was, and still is, to instill an insatiable thirst for more knowledge, slaking that thirst by means of the learning style that most suits you.

I like the way Mark Roche, former dean of the College of Arts and Letters at the University of Notre Dame, describes the characteristics of a liberally educated person. In addition to being free to pursue an education, in our modern times those pursuing a liberal education may expect to experience freedom *from* ignorance and inability, and freedom *to* understand with confidence and to act with consequence—to exercise critical analysis and reasoning, awareness of context and scale; to engage multiple disciplinary perspectives; and to incorporate moral dimensions of issues into their actions—to be able to listen, process, and communicate. Liberal learning imparts a deep and durable and transferable set of knowledge skills suitable to facilitate creativity and agility. By seeking to develop the whole self, the individual seeks to engage in teamwork with others. At least with regard to Roche's first set of abilities characteristic of the liberally educated, it would seem that we would want and even expect our engineers to possess these.

In addition to skills of mental acuity and the agility to listen, discern, reason, and communicate, Roche asserts that the liberally educated person exercises a capacity to enjoy beauty and possibility and process as much as accomplishment. We may or may not agree that this is a necessary or even desirable thing for our engineers and other professionals to master. After all, part of what places biology but not medicine among the liberal arts, or economics but not business, or math and physics but not engineering, is that we expect the primary focus of professional education to be goal oriented to address problems. As patients, we do not want our physicians to be pursuing new understandings about the basic biology of our cancerous tumor. We want them to address it as best they can with the understanding that exists already. We wouldn't expect any more than that of our practicing engineers would we? Or would we?

The third characteristic of the liberally educated, Roche asserts, is that of a character based on an acquired and internally synthesized and owned set of virtues, virtues that express themselves in action, in vocation. This characteristic has a great deal to do with identity and principle. In this regard, liberally educated persons not only can quote extensively from the thoughts and works of others but, more importantly, can say with conviction ideas that they themselves understand and believe. It is less about being a walking encyclopedia and more about being an author. Until we are able to assert our own positions, we do not have a genuine or authentic identity. Until we are able to do so, we are not able to bring the broader perspective of humanity and ethics into our work.

This is a big deal. To the extent that the practice of ethics can be defined as making decisions based on moral principle, it is arguably the liberally educated who are best able to practice ethics. A few of you in the room are old enough to remember Sen. William Proxmire's

Golden Fleece Awards. The late Democratic senator from Wisconsin, who served from 1957 to 1989, had a regular habit of embarrassing government agencies by citing examples of projects and expenses that he felt wasted taxpayer money. One Golden Fleece Award was given for a wrench used in space travel and another for a toilet seat that was a component of a jet bomber, both items costing the government thousands of dollars each, but seemingly indistinguishable from items available at any hardware store for under twenty dollars. In defense of our engineers, I wonder if they were at first perplexed by the senator's criticism. After all, they had produced items that would meet specifications, address the purpose, and solve the problem. They might not have been told that cost, stewardship of the government coffers, was also an important design criterion. In following years addressing other of society's technological needs, engineers would learn that not only cost but also energy efficiency and eventually economic impact and other broader societal considerations would be incorporated into design criteria. But should it have been necessary to point out those values to our engineers and their design teams?

By the way, engineers are not alone in requiring training to be sensitive to the application of moral principle to decisions. A more sinister illustration can be made of the practice of subprime mortgage lending that precipitated the Great Recession. If the design driver had been to expand the mortgage business, there is no question that lucrative new markets were opened by structuring loans for which people could qualify. Never mind that at the end of the day, when the loan payments ballooned, they would have virtually no possibility of carrying the loan to its maturity. It was a clever idea and required significant intellectual capacity. Even more clever, brilliant in fact, was the ability to repackage those loans to sell as high-grade investments to banks and other Wall Street investors. But had the practice of making decisions been based at least in part on moral principle, one would have discovered that the brilliantly defined processes for short-term financial gain were not ethical. Certainly that characteristic of liberal learning that develops a sense of individual identity and core virtues is something we would want not only of our financial leaders but also of our engineers.

Reconsidering the Curriculum

Considering these several characteristics—intellectual agility and mastery of communication, ability to appreciate possibility and process as well as achievement, and development and ownership of virtues—would it not be a good thing for engineers to be thus educated? Should engineers not be more than merely trained, but able to be counted among the ranks of those engaging in, contributing to, and drawing from a rich life of the mind?

You might even contend that men and women educated as engineers already embody these characteristics and may very well have a rightful claim to be called liberal learners. But I doubt that they would identify themselves as such. This brings me to my final set of thoughts. What should our engineering schools be doing both to make explicit the value of liberal learning and to convey the expectation that engineering students will develop the capacities traditionally associated with liberal learners? In terms of curriculum, a Delaware undergraduate degree in electrical or computer engineering already requires six general education requirements (no different than forty years ago) but admirably also requires a course in critical reading and writing, a junior course in English, and a senior course in ethics and the impact of engineering. The curricula at other universities in which I have studied and taught impose a communication requirement, but neither as much nor as visibly as the curriculum here. And neither of those institutions is explicit about the value of ethics in the engineering curriculum. So I have now still another reason to be especially proud of my Delaware degree.

But I am not sure that curricular changes really ensure that engineering students both receive and enjoy the fact that their engineering education may be also a liberal education. We all know that there is very little breathing room in a modern engineering curriculum. Some of us recall that period in the 1980s when the explosion of technical information had educators at their wits' end to figure out how to squeeze everything into a four-year engineering program. That was when MIT experimented with eliminating entirely the bachelor's degree in electrical engineering, offering only a five-year master's. At Dartmouth, the engineering curriculum was shortened to three years, culminating in a general engineering degree without any specialty designation. An additional two years was required for the specialty, and then another five-year program was proposed. Neither experiment ultimately succeeded. Instead, the disciplines decided that students should master engineering fundamentals using the most recent technology to provide examples that reinforce those fundamentals.

So if it is unwise to attempt to augment our curriculum to accommodate every aspect of modern technological advance, what does that say about the desirability of curricular change to facilitate more effective liberal learning through our engineering curriculum? To answer that question, it is instructive to be reminded of the original liberal arts curriculum. By the time the University of Bologna had been established in 1088, so had the formal liberal arts curriculum. It consisted of two parts, the trivium and quadrivium. The trivium included grammar, logic, and rhetoric, while the quadrivium encompassed arithmetic, music, geometry, and astronomy. Only later did the curriculum grow to include history, art, literature, mathematics, the social sciences, physics, chemistry, and biology. Lining up the curricular elements of the trivium and quadrivium against the characteristics that we now associate with those who receive a liberal education, we see that the intellectual skills are addressed explicitly. That is to say that, in 1088, one might have been drilled in logic and debate and grammar to hone reasoning and communication skills. But there were no courses explicitly to broaden perspectives and thought or to exercise ethics and moral reasoning. Presumably, it was expected that these virtues were acquired in the aggregate experience of the education and through exposure to the attitudes and caliber of the faculty as mentors and experts.

Beyond course requirements, and perhaps without even needing to add any new subject matter to the curriculum, we should be encouraged by the earliest roots of our academic institutions to do more to prepare the minds of our students and to sharpen our own. Since engineering exists specifically to have a positive impact on society, could we not entertain in our classrooms and our conversations more of the why questions? What happens when we broaden effective design criteria as widely as possible, rather than narrowing the criteria to help ensure that our students' efforts will converge to a single and simple right answer? You recall the old joke of the physicist called in to address the agriculture board about maximizing food yields, who begins by drawing a circle on the board declaring, "Let's assume a spherical cow." But engineers have the rich challenge of working in the real world, a challenge to take into account every dimension of reality—the physical and behavioral, the known, the unknown, and the unknowable. Is there really any course with a design component that does not also provide the opportunity to have a running conversation about ethics? Is there any laboratory course that doesn't provide almost weekly opportunities to reinforce the value of the ability to write with clarity?

Of course, my entire argument today has been based on the assertion that our discipline has the potential to impart, more fully and deliberately, the skills and disciplines and values that we associate with the liberal learner, and that doing so might better serve our students and our society. If the twofold purpose of a liberal education is first to help students identify and develop how they best learn and secondly to impart an insatiable desire to continue learning, then I personally can attest to the great value of my Delaware engineering degree and the liberal education that I received in pursuing it. It is something for which I will forever be deeply grateful.

Part 3

The Life of the Mind

"Can We Talk?"

Can we talk?

You may remember that that was the line for comedian Joan Rivers. "Can we talk?" What she meant was, can we share some secrets? Can we speak in confidence and trust each other to protect what we have to say? It was a brilliant basis for the rest of her comedy routine.

When I read certain passages from the Hebrew Bible, the same question comes to my mind. Can we talk? But in a different sense. Not just can we talk in general, but are we able to talk about something like wisdom? We don't seem to do it much. We sprinkle the word *wisdom* around, but we don't enter into a meaningful discussion to make us more wise, more aware. Do we even have a language for wisdom? Do we have a foundation for building a shared understanding, shared concepts, or a common experience out of which we can begin to talk?

Some of us might think hopefully that we can talk about anything. But I don't think so. For example: today is Mother's Day. Students, you likely cannot talk the same way about the miracle of childbirth as your parents. There's something so profound about giving birth to possibility and opportunity that unless you have experienced it yourself, we could use all the right words and you still wouldn't get it. You can't really talk about it until you've experienced it, and even then the experience may be inexpressible.

Let me give you another example of how words fail. Imagine talking to a friend who is profoundly color-blind, or in fact unsighted, blind altogether. Can you talk to your friend about color? Can you explain red to someone who has never seen it? How would you do it? The physicist might think of 600 nanometers, and the poets about a warm color, and musicians about the red intensity of some music. And yet if the blind person says, "Okay, 600 nanometers, warm, and intense; now I know red," you would shake your head—no, you don't know red because you haven't experienced it, sadly.

I suspect there are many other matters of the spirit too wonderful for words only. Wisdom may be one of those things. But there is perhaps something that has happened to you after four years of independent living, four years of intense interpersonal and intellectual activity, that you have been able to see something more of the color of wisdom. Is that possible?

One of the principal means by which we experience or encounter wisdom is simply through living. You've done some great living. You've encountered life opportunities that in some cases may seem trivial but challenged you to make wise or unwise choices. You know—choices about how much sleep to get, how much studying to do, what major to choose, what courses to sign up for. Decisions about health—will I exercise, will I smoke, will I drink? You were challenged to make wise choices about friends, activities, and clubs you would join, maybe about future spouses and partners. You have been forced to exercise wisdom, and like all exercise, that has meant using what you have and making it stronger through repeated use.

Other experiences that build wisdom in us are those profound life moments that cause us to reevaluate our priorities. You've had some of those. Maybe it was around a deep and certain calling to a vocation. Maybe it was about the failure of a relationship. Maybe it was a death. Having been through all that, you have been made considerably wiser. You do have some sense of the color of wisdom. So in a way that we couldn't four years ago, before you came here, we *can* talk. We can talk about wisdom. So let's do it.

What is wisdom? My favorite definition of wisdom is the apt use of knowledge. I like that link between knowledge and the appropriate use of it. Of course, knowledge and wisdom are linked often. You probably have noticed, over the last four years, the motto of your alma mater. It is *Cor prudentis possidebit scientiam*, which means—with apologies to Latin scholars—that the prudent heart will acquire knowledge, or as we like to translate it, the wise heart seeks knowledge. It's from Proverbs 18.

So knowledge must be part of wisdom. Knowledge, that accumulation of and facility with facts and philosophies and logic. But knowledge is not sufficient for wisdom.

By the way, Asa Candler would agree with me. The founder of the Coca-Cola Company, he was also the fellow who gave a million dollars to help plant Emory in Atlanta back in 1915. In the letter where he declared his eagerness to do that, dated July 16, 1914, he writes about the relationship between knowledge and wisdom. He says, "In my opinion, the education which sharpens and strengthens the mental faculties without at the same time invigorating the moral powers is a curse rather than a blessing, creating dangerous ambitions and arousing selfish passions faster than it supplies restraints upon these lawless tendencies in human nature."

Asa wouldn't stop with knowledge as the only component of wisdom; he mentioned a moral component. Where does that come from?

The Emory vision statement commits us to being inquiry driven and ethically engaged. Ethics might be defined very simply as making decisions based on moral values. That's where that moral element comes in. Ethics is not a moral code, by this definition. It's rather a process of deliberation and decision making guided by moral principles.

Many of us, but certainly not all, view these as divinely given values that we have by revelation. But revelation also comes from wise counselors, wise mentors, and wise friends. Imagine a moment in your life when you had a particularly grand, mountaintop experience over a personal relationship. Maybe it's a parent-child relationship, maybe it is brother-sister, boyfriend-girlfriend. Think of a particularly high moment, and then allow your mind to rattle off what you associate with that. You might recite words like trust, loyalty, consideration, courtesy. In fact, if I let you keep going, some experts say you'd come up without about 125 such associations before you repeated yourself. That's a set of moral values. Making decisions true to those moral values is ethics.

So ethics is part of that aptness that defines wisdom as the apt use of knowledge—the use of knowledge in a way that fits our moral values.

Yet even this combination of ethics and knowledge does not fully make for a complete understanding of wisdom.

Go back in your mind to the time when you were trying to decide where to come to college—when you finally had narrowed it down to Emory and school B. You could have made a choice based on knowledge. Your choices should be based on knowledge, but a choice made only with data and information is the sort of thing that a computer could do for you. An algorithm could answer the questions whether the college has the major you're interested in, whether it is the size you would be comfortable with, a location you would enjoy, a certain distance from home. These are all numbers and facts that should be part of the knowledge on which you based your decision.

But I know that wasn't enough for you. You wanted to make a wise decision. So then you asked, "Am I making an ethical choice?" For example, would going to an expensive school somehow compromise the ability of a younger sibling to attend college later?

But having answered the ethical question, and having responded with knowledge, you know that something else less tangible entered into making a wise decision. So wisdom must be more than a combination of knowledge and ethics.

Let me suggest that in addition to knowledge, in addition to ethics, wisdom has a component that could be described as impact. To act upon wisdom is to have positive impact—positive impact on individuals, your circumstances, and the community around you. Conversely, great knowledge and moral understanding kept to oneself—well, that's not wise. That would be like having the world's most useful tool and never picking it up.

So we do have a vocabulary we can use to talk about wisdom and the role of knowledge and ethics and the importance of having impact. We can begin to talk about wisdom. We can understand that to be wise is to employ knowledge and ethics for a positive impact on yourself and the world around you. That's a fairly awesome definition of wisdom.

With this definition, I think we can talk. We could start a discussion right now. Some of you may not be so sure. You may not be happy with this notion of positive impact. You may consider yourself a gifted critic who can help the world by a more negative critique of what's wrong with it. Let's talk about that. I'd like to. Or somebody else is saying, "You know, this business about the world around you—I'm not so sure." Shakespeare writes, "This above all, to thine own self be true." Every time you fly on an airplane, the flight attendant says to put the mask on yourself first in an emergency. So there must be something wise and ethical about "me first." What a great discussion we could have now that we have language around wisdom.

It's a discussion that I hope will last a lifetime. Talk from your current store of wisdom, however thin it might feel. Talk and listen to wise friends and mentors to add to your store of wisdom.

And as you leave here, may your experience serve as a true source of all wisdom. May that source be gracious in sharing wisdom with you. May God help you to do well, may God help you to do good, and may God make you wise.

Journey to Emory, Journey to Mars

We humans seem to have a need for liberating our spirits by liberating our feet—for trekking because we believe that experiencing a journey and a different place will lead us to a kind of inner transformation. It's not just any journey or place that will foster this transformation, however. It's not tourism; it's pilgrimage.

For many of us who set out on pilgrimage, this inner need plays out through a determination to connect in a physical way with the spiritual landscape of others. People stand at the site where Pickett's Charge began at Gettysburg not simply to view the landscape but to imagine what thousands of men must have felt like as they faced each other across a mile of fields on July 3, 1863. Christians, Jews, and Muslims travel to Jerusalem not merely to visit particular sites but to try to experience how stony streets and bare hills helped shape a distinctive sense of the holy among the city's ancient peoples. Devotees of Shakespeare journey to his tomb not to touch a piece of marble but to stand as close as possible to the mortal remains of someone they would love to have had a dinner conversation with. Behind the urge to pilgrimage lies a deep, irrational need for an understanding of history, emotion, and transcendence beyond our ordinary experience.

This need is not always about the past, but it is about significance and meaning. Consider a "pilgrimage" to Mars, which would be a significant and meaningful undertaking indeed. Most scientists agree that there is no earthly reason, so to speak, to send a human passenger in a spacecraft to the red planet. Robots could do everything that an astronaut could do there—gather soil samples, test the atmosphere, take photographs—and do it just as well or better. What a robot could not tell us, however, is what it must mean to walk on another planet and know oneself to be almost impossibly cut off from some of the most basic experiences of being human—a vision of blue sky, a feeling of wind on the face, earth under the feet. No robot could feel the poignancy of being human in a place devoid of all signs of human passing or human possibility. Only a pilgrim would understand the significance.

Human beings long to go on pilgrimage for the sake of an outward experience that renders, in the old formula of the sacraments, "an inward grace." We sense that taking ourselves off to a place beyond our ordinary, everyday realm of experience is the prerequisite to deep transformation of our tired or undereducated or parochial selves whom we wish to be no longer. For that reason, going to college will always be an important pilgrimage for some men and women, even if "going" to college means no more than driving across town for evening classes in a building that could be mistaken for an office park or a travel agency.

One reason why great universities like Oxford, Cambridge, and Harvard appeal to prospective students is that they are not only home to superior scholars but also appropriate destinations for pilgrims of the mind: here in Magdalen College at the University of Oxford, C. S. Lewis had his rooms and wrote *The Chronicles of Narnia*; here in the Cavendish Laboratory at the University of Cambridge, Watson and Crick, with the help of Rosalind Franklin's data, mapped the structure of the DNA molecule; here in the First Parish Church near Harvard Yard, Emerson delivered his era-shaping Phi Beta Kappa oration, "The American Scholar." Here in Glenn Memorial, Emory has heard the wisdom of Nobel Prize winners Desmond Tutu, Jimmy Carter, the Dalai Lama, Elie Wiesel, Wole Soyinka, and Seamus Heaney. In breathing the atmosphere of these sites, fitting our spirits temporarily to their architecture and landscape, we perhaps imagine that we participate in some small way in the greatness of heart of those who left their shimmering legacy there.

This enlargement of the self, which is also a transformation of one's understanding, is the principal mission of a university like Emory. At the core of all the research, teaching, service, scholarship, and social action in which Emory people engage daily burns a bright conviction that these are the paths to growth, change, and improvement, to participation in the maturing of humanity—both our personal humanity and humanity in general.

Something innate in the human psyche spurs us to pilgrimage. As long as universities are worthy places for such pilgrimage, they will satisfy that drive, will be necessary, and will flourish.

Astonishment and Wonder

The tradition of the baccalaureate service seems to date to 1432 at the University of Oxford. At those early services, each graduate was required to deliver a sermon—in Latin! Of course, in those days, universities existed primarily to educate ministers, so sermonizing was old hat. Today the baccalaureate is a service of thanksgiving and celebration of successful undergraduate careers. It gives the university community an opportunity to pause, to put into perspective where we have been and where we should be going.

Psalm 19 in the Hebrew Bible records the psalmist's surprise and delight that the heavens tell the glory of God. Without words, the heavens speak volumes. There is excitement in the voice of the psalmist as he acknowledges this. He exults that the firmament (the full visible expanse of the universe) proclaims the intangible wonder of the spiritual.

Those words were written centuries ago, in what we often are tempted to view as less sophisticated, less scientific times. In our own seemingly more advanced day, nothing seems to astonish us. We no longer need to worry about being surprised by wide-eyed wonder. Or do we? Maybe we would do well to be less impressed by our sophistication and more eager to be surprised by wonder in spite of how unsophisticated it might make us feel.

With a modern education from a major research university, no one is better prepared than you to be able to wonder at what the world reveals about things natural and supernatural—to be filled with awe and delight and to be drawn into the virtuous seduction of creative expression and discovery of the unknown. The universe—tangible and intangible, seen and unseen, physical and spiritual—is limitless and is rightly the object of wonder.

And yet, no one is more at risk than you for failing to practice wonder—for believing that the world must be kept to a small, knowable, and manageable size. After all, you have been managing a complicated academic program for four years now and are practiced in keeping things under control. The insistence on being in control in this way not only limits joy in life but also has potentially tragic consequences. Too often in my academic career, I have had the sad experience of helping a university community cope with a loss from suicide. It's not something that you ever get used to. Always you are struck by how small the victim's world had become and how despondent they were that they could not control even a world so small. How horribly ironic it is for this to occur at an institution committed to expanding worlds and horizons. Perhaps we all are at risk—you and I—of failing to wonder. Perhaps all of us in some ways have suppressed our sense of wonder. Has a university education enlarged for us the possibility of wonder and awe, or could our experiences here, paradoxically, have worked to dampen those emotions? Are our worlds too small?

Tomorrow is commencement day. It's a day that marks and celebrates your accomplishments. You will receive gifts. You will receive cards, many of them with checks inside, that congratulate you for what you have done and declare that "today is your day." It's all about you.

These are fine sentiments, but they are hardly an adequate summary of what we really should commemorate at commencement. The exclusive focus on personal accomplishment may be an unfortunate byproduct of an education at a powerful research university. It's entirely understandable that, having experienced for so long the pressure of academic competition, of meeting deadlines, of satisfying requirements, of getting your research done, of completing your thesis or defending your dissertation, of focusing on fitting in socially, you may have missed the fact that Emory has been trying to prepare you for a deeper sense and appreciation of wonder in the face of all that is around and beyond you.

So . . . what is wonder? The dictionary says that it is a feeling stirred by something strange or surprising that prompts you to want to learn more about it. How do we foster these feelings? How do we dwell in this state? Why should we bother to try?

Well, there are practical reasons to foster these feelings and to seek to live in a state of wonder. Albert Einstein wrote about the importance of wonder. He said, "[Those] who can no longer pause to wonder and stand in awe [are] as good as dead; [their] eyes are closed." Emerson declared that human beings "love to wonder, and that is the seed of our science." Socrates remarks, in Plato's *Theatetus*, that "wisdom begins in wonder." To listen to these wise ones tell it, wonder is essential for discovery, creativity, and wisdom.

Secondly, we should practice and refine our abilities to wonder simply because it feels good. The feelings aroused by genuine wonder include awe, delight, and motivation.

"Awe," Rabbi Abraham Heschel tells us, "is an intuition for the dignity of all things." Imagine ascribing to others and to things beyond ourselves the same dignity that we usually reserve for the protection and preservation of our own self-esteem. Watch it—if you truly wonder, it will happen. We all have experienced awe at the prospect of natural beauty, in the heroic acts of others, and in the power of emotion. But usually, we are surprised by it rather than having honed a keen talent for seeking it and the expectation that we should experience it regularly.

Beyond awe, wonder prompts delight. The kind of delight that derives from wonder comes more from a process of seeking, exploring, imagining, and creating than from acquiring or possessing. The delight of wonder is motivated by a certainty that there is more to know—even more to know than we can possibly know.

This notion that seeking may be more delightful than achieving and possessing is apparent in the behavior of young children, in that "wow" stage of discovery when they are toddlers. Everything—every squirrel on the lawn, every toy in the crib, every piece of lint on the carpet—holds a fascination that beckons to be chased, grasped, and, if possible, put in the mouth! The pursuit of discovery, the wonder itself, is a source of joy and delight.

So if wonder is that awesome, delightful, and motivating—if it is that valuable—why do so many of us fail to practice it?

Sadly, as a society, we have picked up some bad habits. Even more sadly, those of us with academic accomplishment under our belts, we who have been given tools and methods to practice and enjoy wonder, are the very ones at greater risk for failing to do so. Some of our failure comes from academic privilege that decays into academic arrogance. Some of it comes from honest fear of what we might discover if we really opened ourselves to explore what the heavens and firmament are telling.

The temptation for us is to feel that we, above others, have the capability, either as individuals or as a species, to understand everything somehow and someday. You would think that such self-confidence would make us all the more curious and filled with wonder. But too often an odd scenario unfolds instead. Our intellectual honesty challenges our self-confidence. We know that there is far too much to comprehend fully, too much to be known (every second of history, every force of nature). But if that is so, then our confidence that everything can be fully known is at risk of being shattered. Our understandable act of intellectual self-defense is to withdraw into what we feel comfortable knowing, to build a wall around it, and to steadfastly resist the temptation to step beyond that wall to what may be outside of our personal universe. We arrest our minds before they escape the comfortable limits of what we think we know, and we thus miss the wonder of things strange and surprising. We avoid the risk that the strange and the surprising might be disquieting and humbling, not delightful. As the late Nobel Prize–winning physicist Richard Feynman might say, we would rather memorize comfortable answers than know wonder.

Many of you will receive master's degrees tomorrow. I am pleased to have you receive a diploma certifying that you have completed advanced study. But the fact that we call it a master's degree is unfortunate. We should not feel for a moment that we are masters of our disciplines and need no longer ask what more there is to know.

If academic arrogance and settling for comfortable answers is one set of bad habits that threaten our ability to practice wonder, another bad habit is "science worship." We do a great deal of that in this country. As a scientist and engineer myself, I love science and technology. Science excites me, and I disagree with Ludwig Wittgenstein, who wrote that we have to "awaken to wonder . . . Science is a way of sending [us] off to sleep again." But I can see how he might have concluded that. Consider some examples of science worship.

In our so-called scientific times, we ascribe reality primarily to things that can be measured through the effect they have on our environment. We have scientific metrics for mass and energy. Less scientifically, yet nevertheless real, are emotions like love and hate, and matters of faith and spirit.

We worship experts and excuse ourselves for not wondering about what lies beyond their expertise. Experts deserve respect, but real experts long to be engaged and confronted, not believed unquestioningly.

Another wonder-blocker is rigidity and routine. Routine can serve positively to comfort and focus us, as in religious ritual. On the other hand, routine can confine us to the familiar—anathema to things strange and surprising, to wonder. To stay in that habitually comfortable space develops in us the bad habit of ignoring things beyond us. And ignoring is perhaps the worst thing we can do to each other and to the universe.

Consider the psalmist celebrating that "the heavens are telling the glory of God and the wonder of God's works." Contrast that with the passage in the Book of Revelation, where God is heard saying that hot and cold are infinitely better than lukewarm. God is saying, "I wish you could feverishly embrace me or coldly but diligently apply yourself to deny and disprove me. But engage me, do not be lukewarm and ignore me. Wonder about me!"

Perhaps you and I can see in ourselves one or more of these bad habits that block the enjoyment of wonder in our lives. But if there are habits and practices that block wonder, there are also ways that we can foster it.

The delightful journey of wonder is not always about the present. Sometimes it is about the past. Professor Don Saliers, of the Candler School of Theology, writes in his book *Worship Come to Its Senses* about a retreat with a group of Emory students. At a particular moment, he asked if they could share an example of a meal they had eaten that held a significant memory. A shy sophomore woman responded. As Don tells it, "She described a Thanksgiving meal at her grandmother's house.

After speaking of the details of the table and the conversation, she quietly added, 'And that was the last time that I ate with my grandmother and grandfather.'" This young woman could not have known that it would be the last meal she would ever share with her grandparents. But it was a memory worth revisiting. In reflection, she could wonder over it. So the habit of reflection fosters wonder.

Another discipline for building a facility for wonder is to be aware of revelation. That is exactly what the psalmist is doing when he declares that the heavens are telling the glory of God. This discipline requires us to look up from the focus of the immediate and take in a broader vista. We increase the scope of our view, but we diminish our own relative significance. It is a challenge to become comfortable with such humility. It requires becoming more like that child I spoke about earlier, delighted and unafraid that the world is boundless and not fully knowable.

Fostering a sense of wonder by pausing for reflection and opening to revelation requires another, more critical discipline: faith. It is difficult to imagine how one could fully embrace wonder, either to celebrate it in art or to grasp at understanding through science, without faith. So long as we insist on keeping at least one foot in what we suppose to be our comfort zone, we may never allow ourselves to explore with abandon beyond ourselves and encounter the deep delight of wonder. We are at times like children who cling to the side of the swimming pool for fear that we will sink if we let go. As a result, we do not allow ourselves the joy of floating and splashing and being buoyed up by a force that we may not have experienced before. Fear, and not faith, rules our day.

C. S. Lewis made the same point in a more illustrative way when he wrote that it is difficult to convince children (like us) who are enjoying making mud pies in a vacant inner-city lot just how much more fun we might have at the seashore. Present comforts and the inability to imagine restrain us from using faith and courage to reach for greater knowledge and freedom. When we wonder faithfully, we bravely and deeply encounter matters not only of the physical world but also of the spiritual world.

Reflection, openness to revelation, and faith are keys to wonder. And you, young scholars, are among those most able to wonder—to experience awe, to be delighted, and to be motivated. In doing so, you will become truly educated.

Perhaps too often, some of you have heard me remind you that the true marks of a liberal education are, first, the ability to learn, honed in your own style by formal education and, second, an insatiable appetite to learn more–in other words, to wonder. Without wonder, you will have acquired only half of what a liberal education is intended to provide.

So as I said, tomorrow will be a wonderful day. It's a day that marks your accomplishments. But it's really about remembering that you have been taught to see what others see, feel what others feel, learn what others know, seek to discover what more there is to know, and listen to the heavens. You have been taught to use your potential to reach beyond yourselves, to exercise and grow in faith, to seek to know and serve something far greater than yourselves, and to delight in wonder.

Baccalaureate Address, May 10, 2009

Thinking about Abundance in a Time of Scarcity

A baccalaureate message is an attempt to call out, from the interstices of your experiences at Emory, lessons that you already have learned, ways in which you have grown but may not yet have labeled and typed into your mental transcripts. To speak this year about abundance, in the wake of the biggest financial crisis since the Great Depression, may seem odd. Many in the world are experiencing deep scarcity. Maybe we should be talking about sacrifice. But abundance is something you have experienced in ways that transcend bank statements, housing markets, job markets, and other material measures.

It is in times of constraint and confusion that we most often turn to the inspired reflections of others, to the wisdom found in biographies and sacred scripture, among other places. The Christian apostle Paul offers one such source. In his letter to the Philippians, he encourages us to acquire the discipline of thinking on "whatever is true, whatever is honorable, whatever is just, whatever is pure, whatever is pleasing, whatever is commendable." You may recognize these words, by the way, from the inscription on the fountain in the Goizueta Business School's Patterson Green. Paul goes on to write, "if there is any excellence, anything worthy of praise, think about these things."

That sounds easy. And who would not want to give thought to high-minded things? But Paul is asking us to do more than attend to "feel-good" subjects. He is reminding us that disciplined thinking about these particular things lies at the root of full and abundant lives.

Whatever is true, honorable, just, pure, pleasing, commendable, excellent, praiseworthy: there is a real challenge in trying to dwell on these things, because it is not our first instinct and does not come naturally. Our natural inclination often seems to be toward criticism, toward focusing on the negative. I don't know if this tendency is genetic or acquired and cultivated. Wild animals seem to assume the worst in other species, including humans, and flee from presumed predators—part of their genetically selected-for survival instinct. But I suspect that our own critical selves are the products of years of education and cultivation. Critique, after all, is a legitimate and necessary component of literary, historical, artistic, and scientific practice.

But criticism that goes beyond well-honed analysis seems to have become an overused tool in our time, verging on cynicism and cruelty. We seem to gain personal satisfaction from the defeat of someone else's idea, or from bursting someone's bubble, or from the exposure of others' foibles and failures. It's as though we harbor the illusion, as my father used to warn me, that our own candles shine more brightly if we extinguish the light from those around us. Criticism—again, not to be confused with necessary critical analysis, but attack intended to diminish the persons and ideas of others—is now highly refined. Public criticism is a mainstay of evening talk shows, so-called mockumentaries, political campaign advertising, and even investigative journalism. We like to "bring 'em down." But that widely practiced, and widely laughed-with, form of criticism is the antithesis of abundant thinking and living. Instead of reflecting on what is true, honorable, just, pure, pleasing, commendable, excellent, and praiseworthy, we find it seductively more fun to focus on whatever or whoever is vulnerable, imprecise, imperfect, unpatriotic, disloyal, uncultured, unaware.

Our intentions may be good. After all, there is something noble about wanting to correct all of the wrong in the world. But even with good intentions, when we focus on fixing what's broken, we discover that we are like the crew of a sinking ship working hard belowdecks to caulk and repair every leak. The ship might indeed stay afloat, but with no one on deck to guide it, the vessel will merely drift. The absence of flaws alone does not accomplish a purpose.

Some of you may have had a class with or enjoyed a lecture by Professor Corey Keyes in our Sociology Department. Corey researches the field of psychological well-being. He writes as though he has read Paul's words on abundance. He clearly dislikes the notion that the opposite of depression is nondepression. Instead, he proposes that the opposite of mental illness and languishing is mental health and flourishing. *Flourishing*—what a great word. He even has developed thirteen "symptoms" that indicate when people are "afflicted" with flourishing. These symptoms include having a positive attitude toward others while acknowledging their difference and complexity; exhibiting self-direction; having a sense of autonomy; accepting themselves for who they are. You get the idea.

So we begin to understand that there are measures for abundance, for flourishing, and that Paul is not offering just a sunny platitude. To think on these things calls for deliberate effort. You have heard this before from the Dalai Lama, who visited Emory in his role of Presidential Distinguished Professor in the fall of your junior year. From the Tibetan Buddhist tradition of compassion meditation, being studied at Emory for its positive effect on depression, we learn that we can achieve greater flourishing by thinking on these things with practice and attention.

It may seem counterintuitive, though, to think that we can pursue happiness by developing a sense of abundance even amid evident scarcity. We often believe that events or behaviors outside us might *make* us happy and full. We imagine that perhaps abundance can be inherited or won in the lottery or experienced at a vacation resort or found in the arms of a lover. But wisdom suggests that it is not present circumstance but rather a certain discipline of the mind that brings fullness and abundance. To experience abundance, we must do more than simply take the time to smell the roses during good times; we must have courage and discipline to think on the best of things during stormy periods.

Your time at Emory has been marked by stormy periods, beginning with your arrival here just as Hurricane Katrina hit the Gulf Coast and ending with the economic storm that is upon us. We all have experienced personal storms that perhaps no one but ourselves will ever know about. There will be more storms breaking in our futures. There has been and will continue to be ample opportunity to focus on storms.

But even as we may be forced to attend to difficulties, we can secure an awareness of deep abundance through mental discipline and serious work. I am not suggesting that we approach life solemnly—just seriously. The great Samuel Johnson writes that "the size of a [person's] understanding may be justly measured by [their] mirth." C. S. Lewis, in his essay *The Weight of Glory*, writes that while life must be taken seriously, "This does not mean that we are to be perpetually solemn. We must play. But our merriment must be of that kind (and it is, in fact, the merriest kind) which exists between people who have, from the outset, taken each other seriously."

So while the pursuit of a sense of abundance in times of scarcity is unnatural and counterintuitive, and while it requires mental discipline and serious work, and while it carries the risk of embarrassment, it may be that only by faith in the inspirer of all truth can we hope to have the courage to pursue this kind of abundance.

So as you go from this place, may you have the courage and faith to encounter each new situation as an opportunity for adventure, inspiration, and learning—not threat. And from this university, may you take some memory of what is true, what is honorable, what is just, what is pure, what is pleasing, what is commendable, what is excellent, and what is praiseworthy, so that in all circumstances you may think on these things and experience a truly abundant life.

Uncertainty and Enlightenment

For the past four years or so, you graduating students have spent your time at Emory being graded on the accuracy of your work, the precision of your expression, the logic of your argument, and your mastery of facts. You've been urged to be firm in your opinions, stand up for convictions, have confidence in what you know to be true. You've been cautioned to be skeptical of those who don't know the facts, who can't argue for their position, who are soft on the issues. Confidence and certainty are valued. Old myths are to be exploded and replaced with the truth. You will be nobody's fool. An education at a great research university has ensured that you are well down the path of enlightenment.

This morning, though, I want to talk about uncertainty—seemingly the antithesis of all that you have been taught. I want to suggest that all of us would do well to develop a sense of uncertainty to complement that enlightenment that we are supposed to have gained from our education. For we will always have uncertainty with us. The pool of what can be known actually expands as we know more. Oddly, gaining knowledge also enlarges our sphere of ignorance.

Just as knowledge and reason are necessary to deal in the realm of the certain, so wisdom and faith are necessary for navigating the realm of the uncertain, the unknown, the ambiguous. Indeed, a proper embrace of uncertainty can motivate us to explore and discover, can deepen our appetite for wisdom. The bright side of uncertainty is that it can move us to discovery or creativity. "I wish I knew the cause of Alzheimer's disease." "I wish I knew for certain if there were life on Mars."

The darker side of uncertainty is that it often makes us anxious—"I wish I could be certain what he was thinking." "I wish I could be certain of what will be on the exam." "I wish I knew whom to vote for." We are often uncomfortable with that kind of uncertainty. We like things black or white; gray makes us uneasy. We like bumper stickers that offer political, social, and religious certainty in short, pithy, absolute phrases. We like sound bites without embellishment. Subtlety and nuance sometimes disturb us. We like our minds to be made up, and we like to feel in control.

Remarkably often we succumb to the seductive comforts of certainty. Drew Westen, director of clinical psychology at Emory, has confirmed this phenomenon. Drew's study of brain scans shows that most of us shut off the rational elements of our brain when we "discuss" topics that involve our settled political prejudices. Presumably, we are so certain in our position—so comfortable with it—that we close ourselves to the reasoning of others.

The history of science is rife with examples of great and enlightened minds bringing progress in science screeching to a halt when they have made a major discovery or completed a tidy theory that makes them comfortable. Galen, the first-century physiologist, is credited with introducing experimental medicine, but his incorrect assumptions about the function of vital organs like the liver and the heart were held unquestioned until 1,500 years later, when the sixteenth-century scientist Vesalius came along.

Newton was a scientific bully. He was so certain of his theories about the nature of light that he sought to suppress alternative views, which were not published until well after his death.

The list of the crippling effects of certainty goes on and on. The truth is that we must be suspicious of certainty to avoid being trapped in a small, comfortable reality. It is not enough to be driven to discovery by the uncertainty that naturally confronts us; we must develop enough uncertainty about things that we are driven to creative conjecture and experiment. Uncertainty can draw us into discovery.

But how does uncertainty lead to wisdom?

The physicist Mano Singham, in his book *Quest for Truth*, argues that great achievements in science and technology, although made in the pursuit of truth and reality, are actually about exercising control over our immediate environment. Singham says that we really have no chance of discovering an ultimate or objective reality.

Note that this same sentiment is reflected in scripture, written by even wiser and more inspired writers than Dr. Singham. In the story of Job, a man appears to be a pawn in a contest between God and Satan. God is betting that Job is so faithful a servant that, even in the face of the worst fortune that Satan can conjure, Job will not curse God. Job does, however, try to reason about his plight. God's answer to Job is to tell him not to try to understand things beyond his comprehension. And God is pretty blunt. "Who is it that darkens my counsel with words without knowledge? . . . Have you comprehended the vast expanses of the earth? . . . Do you know the laws of the heavens? . . . Who endowed the heart with wisdom or gave understanding to the mind?" The implied answer is that some truths are beyond Job and beyond all of us.

The apostle Paul, likewise, writes that in this life we can only see in a mirror dimly. Paul is probably referring to some hand-polished piece of first-century bronze that distorts color and shape. The best we can hope for is a partial view of reality.

Even scientists know that their work is more about control and self-consistency and less about a clearly understood objective reality. They know that we are viewing life through a foggy window.

Consider what is required of a good scientific theory. Interestingly, only three things:

1. That the theory be consistent with currently observed phenomena;
2. That the theory be able to predict outcomes in the future or under altered conditions; and
3. That the theory be "falsifiable"—that one can conceive of a test that would disprove the theory.

There is absolutely no requirement that a good theory needs to be based on reality! One of the most elegant and accurate mathematical descriptions for electromagnetic field phenomena, Maxwell's equations, is based upon an entirely false assumption. Maxwell's equations assume that the universe is permeated by an ether upon which light and other electromagnetic waves are carried. But there is no such ether.

Newton's law of gravitational force appears similarly to be based on a false reality (certainly if Einstein is correct), but it was good enough to put men on the moon.

The list goes on, of remarkable and useful understanding that is not necessarily a perfect description of reality. The temptation always is to draw false conclusions about what is real. Because Maxwell's equations work, there must be an ether. And because we can successfully put men on the moon with Newton's laws, gravity must be simply an attractive force. Because there are presents under the tree on Christmas morning, there must be a Santa Claus. We can gain a greater measure of certainty and control through our theories, yet even so, science itself implies a deep uncertainty about ultimate truth and reality.

Quantum mechanics, the most successful theory in the history of humankind, not only allows for some uncertainty; it actually requires uncertainty. String theory produces even more useful results but requires the existence of at least five parallel universes. Scientists discussing these matters admit aloud that they are not certain whether they are pursuing science or philosophy or religion.

So how are we going to deal with all of this uncertainty? How can we know what we believe anymore?

With that question, we enter the realm of faith—a concept that is old-fashioned and linked in some people's way of thinking to superstition. Still, let's talk about it.

Paul writes that "faith is being sure of what we hope for and certain of what we do not see." It is a state of mind that places trust or confidence in someone or something.

Faith seems to be in disrepute these days. Placing faith in an individual—say, a political candidate—is bound to lead to disappointment. Faith as a religious term often is linked with exclusionary or oppressive practices. In general, we are often uncomfortable with faith in public, and consequently, we sometimes fear to admit that we exercise it. But all of us do. In fact, faith—that certainty about things we do not see—is a common element in our lives. Consider aspirin. In all the years since the introduction of its trademark name in 1899, we have yet to discover completely the actual pathways by which aspirin relieves headache. We take aspirin for our headaches not because of any certainty of science but because of faith in the testimony of witnesses who have gone before us and faith in our own experience. You exercise faith and, under some circumstances, are comfortable with it.

Now faith in aspirin might be only a placeholder for our gap in knowledge. Someday, very likely, that gap in our knowledge will be filled when we learn for sure how aspirin works. People of religious faith often argue for the existence of God by saying that the universe is too vast and complex to be fully comprehended, so a master intelligence must exist. Of course, this reduces God to whatever fills the gaps in human knowledge, so that as those gaps are filled, the sense of a transcendent and divine being is diminished.

As quantum mechanics shows, however, there will always be unknowable reality. The unknown and the unknowable are essential to our experience. Dr. Greg Berns, associate professor of psychiatry and behavioral sciences at Emory and author of the book *Satisfaction*, tells us that true satisfaction comes not from mastery and omniscience but from challenge, discovery, and novelty. Presumably when people express strong satisfaction in their marriage after decades together, they are providing evidence that they have not yet come to know all there is to know about their partner, and happily, they never will.

So what do we do with the assurance that there will always be more to know and that we need to exercise faith until we know it? In the same way that we have developed tools of reason to fashion the things we know with certainty, we should develop tools of wisdom to deal with all that is uncertain. It will be with wisdom acting through faith, and not technology and intellect alone, that we will address society's biggest problems of peace, health, and equity. And such wisdom comes from embracing uncertainty:

- uncertainty that keeps open a sense of possibility and an eagerness to discover;

- uncertainty that requires judgment in how we practice our careers and callings;
- uncertainty that keeps open channels of communication on subjects that make us uncomfortable;
- uncertainty that does not freeze us in fear of the unknown but calls faith into practice to provide comfort, courage, and power.

You have been at Emory for four years. During that time, we have worked hard, as you have, to exchange what we can of the little knowledge that we have and the tools of reason and even some wisdom to help you on your way. My wish for all of you, in addition to the blessings that you have secured at Emory—the blessings of knowledge and reason, of literary and artistic expression, and of relationships and community—my wish is that God will bless you with

the freedom of uncertainty;
the love of wisdom; and
the courage of faith.

Part 4

A Community of Character

Charity in a Different Light

I want to talk with you about charity. I do not mean the sort of charity to which you donate money. Instead, I mean a discipline of character and community. Perhaps the word "charitableness" captures better the virtue I have in mind.

For many, the word "charity" may be familiar as part of Christian wedding ceremonies. The so-called "Love Chapter" of the apostle Paul's first letter to the Corinthians often is read at these moments. You know the passage: "Love is patient, love is kind." The passage would sound less familiar if you read from the four-century-old King James translation, which instead of the word "love" uses "charity." "And now abideth faith, hope, charity, these three; but the greatest of these is charity." It sounds a bit strange to our ears, but "charity" may be the better choice of words. Because the original Greek word for the sort of love about which Paul is writing is *agape*. That word, translated into Latin as *caritas*, gave us *charity*. But just what is so special about charity that among faith, hope, and charitable love, the greatest is charity?

Well, consider this experience. In January 2012, I had the pleasure to participate in one of the evening events at a weeklong retreat involving about sixty-five Emory students—a retreat called LeaderShape. This is a fantastic program that challenges participants to examine what leadership means and how they might exercise it themselves for the good of others.

Before dinner that evening, we were invited to review sixty-some sheets of newsprint taped on the walls around the large room in the retreat center. Each student had imagined what the newspaper front page might look like on the morning after utopia had been achieved.

The headlines read "War Ended!" and "Hunger Eliminated" and "Illness Eradicated." And the list went on, many of the headlines following this same format. The students had imagined and defined utopia according to the negatives that would be absent in the future rather than in terms of the positive or even glorious circumstances that would be present. Instead of the headline reading "Peace Arrives," it read "War Is Ended." Instead of "Health Is Achieved," it read "Illness Is Eradicated." The tendency to imagine that good is merely the absence of evil is fairly common, and it allows us to settle for too low a standard for measuring progress toward utopia.

Consider another exercise. Suppose I were to ask you to define or describe the very best you. Not the very best that you have been but the very best that you could be. It wouldn't be surprising if a number of you concluded that the best possible you or the best possible me would be someone who is unselfish, un-self-centered, un-self-focused. Once again, though, the desirable quality would be the absence of the undesirable, in this case the absence of selfishness. But the passage that I quoted from Paul says that the greatest virtue is charity. What is the difference?

One answer is that unselfishness is not wanting good things just for me, while charity is a positive, active desire for good things for others. The difference is important. Charity is active; it works for the good for others. Imagine a world in which we would not only (unselfishly) make room for others in our space but actively (charitably) welcome them; where, beyond securing our own lives in a sustainable way, we would try to ensure that others could enjoy some of the sustained bounty; where differences aren't just politely ignored (in the name of an unselfish live-and-let-live philosophy) but are actively engaged and explored in a charitable interest about the other; where conflicts of opinion draw people into discussion rather than drive them to opposite corners of a boxing ring (or opposite sides of the aisles of Congress); where our first reaction to the mistakes and flaws in others is not to ignore or attack, but to want to understand and possibly forgive. Wouldn't we all want to live among those people in that community?

But charity thus understood is hard work. Still—you have done it. You have overcome fears and anxieties, the sorts of things that tend to make charity especially difficult. Indeed, when you think about it, fear may be the single greatest driver for self-centered and selfish behavior—the opposite of charity. Fear prompts a panic of everyone for themselves. To succumb to fear is to abandon charity.

Besides fear, our sometimes wobbly self-confidence can work against the exercise of charity. It seems to be a human characteristic to look for the flaws in and difficulties of others. Whether in our news media or social media, the tendency to focus on the mistakes of others often seems prompted by insecurity about our own bold plans or humble opinions, which might prove to have their own imperfections. Whether mainline news, late-night comedy, or social media postings, so much seems to be offered at the expense of someone else, not for edification—not charitably. We admire the witty critics and repeat their criticisms. Sadly, we seem to take joy in the public embarrassment of others, whether deserving or undeserving. But feeling better about ourselves by highlighting the troubles of others is not charitable—it is not our best selves. It is easier to live with polarization and disunity than to charitably invite engagement, debate, and moderation. To this point, William Penn once said, "Happy would it be if where unity ends, charity did begin." At the point where we disagree, it would be charitable to assume each other's good intentions.

But here is an interesting thing. The final phrase of that passage in 1 Corinthians says, "There is no fear in love (charity). But perfect charity drives out fear." In other words, while fear of vulnerability or anxiety about our ability might make us less prone to exercise charity, charity is at the same time the antidote to that fear, the assurance that we needn't be anxious. Wanting and working for the good of another is a recipe for the defeat of fear. You actually know this to be true. You have experienced this.

Think back to your days of freshman orientation. Very few of you would describe that time as carefree. In fact, if you are honest, you will recall that your early days on campus were a period of anxiety and fearfulness. You weren't always sure what was going on, weren't always sure you were going to fit in, weren't always certain you could make it. Curiously and importantly, though, it was also a moment when many of you made friends who have remained some of your strongest friends throughout your years at Emory, friends who are likely to remain yours for life. How do you explain that?

I suggest that the answer lies in the way fear was subdued by your practice of charity. For a time in those early days, each person you met held the possibility that they could be your friend based on what you had in common, how you enjoyed sharing stories of your backgrounds, and how you explored together the new experiences of academic life. Frankly, you were probably not too selective. All that mattered was that in charity you engaged with kindness and tolerance.

You have learned other lessons of charity here. Many of you can cite examples from community, clubs, and Greek brotherhoods and sisterhoods on campus, or service opportunities off campus and around the world, where you have been both the recipient and the giver of charitable kindness. These experiences have felt wonderful. Some of you even talk about them as life changing. You have exercised the disciplines of mind and heart that give you greater potential than most to be examples of charity in the world, to help others, and to wipe out their fears.

If we at Emory have succeeded in our intent to educate both the heart and the mind, you leave here with the ability and desire for rich enjoyment for yourself and others. You leave here with an unquenchable curiosity, along with the confidence in your ability to learn. You have developed the capacity to view the world from someone else's perspective and to draw on history to shape decisions and predict the impact of your actions. You can envision possibility and not yield to desperation. In short, through all of these disciplines of the mind, you will guide yourself and others by invitation and charity rather than by coercion or cynicism or fear.

Perhaps all of this seems like a lot to remember—this argument that charity is not some activity worthy of a merit badge, but instead a personal discipline for joy and a weapon against fear. Here's a simple way to remember it. The story is told that when Rabbi Hillel was asked to summarize the entire Torah while standing on one foot, he replied famously, "That which is despicable to you, do not do to your fellow. This is the whole Torah, and the rest is commentary. Go and learn it." In the

Christian New Testament, the words of Jesus derive from Hillel in what we know as the golden rule: "Do unto others as you would have them do unto you." While the golden rule might seem like little more than a nursery exhortation from your parents and elementary school teachers, most of us would not need to go back in our memories very many days or perhaps hours to find an example where that rule could have helped us. But to be committed to and guided by that rule is to undertake the hard work of exercising the powerful weapon of charity.

Thus my prayer for you is that of all that you will lean on to guide and sustain you, of all the options that you consider to place in the center of your lives, of all the great intellectual riches and power that you have amassed here—my prayer is that you always will draw strength from faith and hope and charity, discovering and teaching others that the greatest of these is charity.

Character Education

Those looking for a good read might do no better than to pick up a book by David Brooks, *The Road to Character*. Known as a conservative-leaning pundit who writes regularly for the *New York Times* op-ed pages, he keeps politics pretty much out of this book and instead demonstrates a remarkable range of reading across the disciplines of history, theology, psychology, philosophy, and literature. The point of his argument is simple: we develop character through internal struggle against our besetting personal weaknesses. Brooks tests and elaborates that argument through illustrative biographies of exemplary historical figures.

These are not saints (okay—one of them, Saint Augustine, actually is), but they are mortals who had to work to overcome an array of obstacles and harmful susceptibilities. In the process, they forged what Brooks calls character: "a set of dispositions, desires, and habits that are slowly engraved during the struggle against your own weakness." In this view, "character" is not measurable by external achievements. Rather, character is the result of wrestling with deeply personal moral questions that lead one to a vocation in the noblest sense of that word—a calling that matches one's gifts and talents with the world's needs.

The book advances an ancient and well-pedigreed understanding of how moral judgment is formed. But two quotations in the book bring the thesis home for anyone involved in education. The first is by Mary Woolley, one of the first female graduates of Brown University and a president of Mount Holyoke College in the early twentieth century. She wrote, "Character is the main object for education." The second quotation is from the British philosopher Alfred North Whitehead: "Moral education is impossible without the habitual vision of greatness."

What I find provocative about Brooks's book is its implications about the role of educational institutions. Emory has a long history of thinking about education in moral terms. President Emeritus Jim Laney spoke and wrote often and eloquently of "the education of the heart" and the need to develop a "life" rather than a "lifestyle." Nineteenth-century president Atticus Haygood spoke of standing by "what is good" and trying to make the good better—suggesting that judgment and character must be exercised to this purpose. Most recently, our vision statement holds out the prospect of Emory as an "ethically engaged" community.

There is a danger inherent in this kind of language. It suggests to some listeners a kind of piety or self-importance that risks being called out for hypocrisy or cynicism when the institution falters.

Many educators therefore prefer not to push too far in the direction of the moral dimensions of education. Or, rather, they want to insist that whatever moral functions education has are limited to the honor code: "I will not lie, cheat, or steal or tolerate others who do." This restriction of moral purpose is the position of the well-known pundit and scholar Stanley Fish, who has written extensively about higher education from his decades of experience as a literary scholar, teacher, and dean.

In his 2008 book *Save the World on Your Own Time*, Fish insists that academic professionals—the women and men who teach the students, write the books, and run the labs—have only one job, and that is to introduce a new generation to a body of knowledge and to the intellectual tools for analyzing and managing that knowledge. Political and moral views—whether of the Left or the Right or somewhere off the scale—have no place in the classroom except as ideas to be analyzed structurally, studied historically, measured sociologically, and so on; ideas are not held up in the classroom for recruitment of new disciples. Nor, for that matter, should any university have "a position" on a host of policy issues. Fish approvingly quotes a provost who, when asked about his university's position on a particular matter of world affairs, said that the university "has no foreign policy."

Among the descriptions of college that Fish finds repugnant is the phrase "transformative experience"—believing, as he does, that the only transformation worthy of a college is the one that occurs when a student comes to understand an algorithm, a lab procedure, an era of intellectual history, a closely argued reading of a poem.

Fish's position has a lot to recommend it, and as an argument for what professors ought to be doing, I agree with it. But he misses a lot of what a residential liberal arts university like Emory is about. Inside the classroom, his rules should apply. But a campus of nearly 15,000 students and more than 28,000 faculty and staff members is a complex community that needs to order itself to be able to function.

At Emory, we have spent a lot of thought and energy and time thinking about how to order our community of scholars. Through our Class and Labor Committee, our Advisory Committee on Community and Diversity, our Respect Program, our Emory Healthcare Pledge, and other measures, we attempt to hold up that "habitual vision of greatness" that Whitehead suggests is the foundation of moral education. We are not indoctrinating students into a particular set of moral values. But I hope that we are encouraging them to explore the possibility of developing a character worthy of Emory's vision.

Baccalaureate Address, May 13, 2012

Forging an Authentic Identity

The "wisdom literature" of the Hebrew Bible is called that because of the lasting lessons and truths to be found in it—the wisdom it contains. Psalm 139, for instance, which we read at every baccalaureate service at Emory, is part of that genre. The psalmist, by tradition King David, speaks to God, saying, "You have known me." He does not say you have known my people or you have known my family. He says you have known *me*. I have an individual personal identity about which I may not even be fully aware, but you have known me to my depths. The psalmist goes on to say that God would know him or any of us wherever we might try to hide.

That suggests two points: first, that God is all-knowing and ever present, and second, that even so, we might contemplate hiding our authentic selves from God—that for some reason, hiding is an attractive option for us. Maybe we can identify with this thought that there is a real us whom we are not always entirely comfortable with others knowing. In fact, there are times when we put more energy into hiding who we are than having the courage to be fully ourselves.

So we hide. There are many ways and many pressures for us to hide. But one of the lessons and blessings of the university experience has been the low risk associated with openly becoming and being who you are. You came here shaped by home and childhood, and perhaps for some of you, home is still where you feel most free to be who you are. But for others—most, I hope—Emory has provided greater freedom to be known. You may soon enter a new environment where exercising that freedom to develop and display an authentic identity may be more difficult. I urge you not to bend under the pressures to hide or to conform.

Not only would that rob you of freedom, but it would also rob society of the chance to benefit from an authentic you. As the apostle Paul writes in 1 Corinthians, the body is made up of many parts, and each part is valuable and necessary. A healthy community, like a healthy body, requires all of its parts not to wish to be like any of the others, but to function powerfully in their respective and authentic ways.

Maybe the best defense against suppressing our authentic identity might be to consider the ways that we might be tempted to hide it. Sometimes we might choose almost literally to go into hiding, to become reclusive, to keep to ourselves, to exist as loners. But another more common and insidious practice of hiding comes from doing just the opposite. We often hide by joining—by joining political parties, religious groups, or social movements, not because we share with them an identity that we have already authentically developed, but because we believe that joining them can *give* us an identity, even a sense of family. Of course, joining a group can be a powerful way to lend one's identity to a greater cause. But we should join because we have first formed an identity, not because we need one—because we know who we are, because our integrity aligns our own deeply held values with those of the group.

Besides the social pressures to hide our true selves, there is sometimes financial pressure—when our job might depend on taking a certain opinion or association. It troubles me, for instance, when I hear politicians say that they are trying to do what the American people want. In fact, America's system of government—a democratically elected republic—is one whereby we trust our politicians to do what the American people *need*, not simply what we imagine we want. Without an authentic identity of their own, our politicians are tempted to govern by opinion polls to ensure that they can maintain their membership in the clubhouse on Capitol Hill.

So how do you assert and continue to grow an authentic identity without either hiding or selling out, especially as you enter a new environment where staying true to your identity may be more difficult than hiding it or borrowing another? And after all, what is an authentic identity?

A couple of years ago, Mark Roche, former dean of the College of Arts and Letters at the University of Notre Dame, wrote in his book

Why Choose the Liberal Arts that the value of a liberal arts education must go beyond the disciplines of the mind associated with critical thinking. It must have also a moral and social purpose with "the goal of helping students develop virtues, build character, and gain a sense of vocation." I like to think that at Emory, the opportunity to acquire a moral foundation on which to act ethically would be somewhat higher than is reflected in the nationwide Faculty Survey of Student Engagement in 2009. In that survey, 93 percent of faculty respondents teaching at liberal arts institutions said that there should be "quite a bit" or "very much" emphasis on "thinking critically and analytically." That much is right and makes sense, it seems to me. But only 50 percent indicated that there should be "quite a bit" or "very much" emphasis on helping students develop "a personal code of values and ethics." Yet it is by adopting a deeply held code of values and ethics that we develop the basis to define ourselves and set our goals and respond to the opportunities and challenges presented by life. Without this personal code, this authentic identity, we are relegated to making choices based on our longing to belong. Failing to bring authentic selves to life, we mostly take from our groups rather than contribute creatively to them.

In his book *Half Time*, Bob Buford challenges his readers to name that one thing or one set of virtues and values that are the central motivator in their lives. He reminds us of the character Curly in the 1991 movie *City Slickers*, starring Billy Crystal and Jack Palance. The story is about a group of thirty-something yuppies who sign up to ride on a cattle drive and use the experience to examine their lives. Billy Crystal plays the lead city fellow, Mitch, and Jack Palance plays Curly, the weathered and crusty cowboy who serves as the guide on this adventure. Mitch describes Curly as leathery, "a saddlebag with eyes," he says. Curly is rugged and intimidating. (Mitch: "Good morning, Curly. Killed anyone today?" Curly: "Today ain't over yet.") But Curly is also wise. At one point, out on the range, when the conversation becomes philosophical, there's this exchange.

CURLY: Do you know what the secret of life is?
[holds up one finger]

CURLY: This.

MITCH: Your finger?

CURLY: One thing. Just one thing. You stick to that and the rest don't mean [anything].

MITCH: But, what is the "one thing?"

CURLY: [smiles] That's what *you* have to find out.

Again, the apostle Paul writes, "But *one thing* I do: Forgetting what is behind and straining toward what is ahead, I press on toward the goal to win the prize for which God has called me."

Whether it's Mark Roche, Bob Buford, Curly, or Paul, all seem to be urging us to examine our lives to ensure that we have in place the central thing that defines our identity. They challenge us to find and place just one thing in the center of our being so that everything else is second. That one thing in the center could be borrowed from those groups that we would like to join. It could be popularity, fame, wealth, or recognition. And you can see how making those things central would define your identity clearly and crisply as well as determine your choices about the opportunities and issues you face. That one thing could be more noble, like family and community and country. But the sources of wisdom suggest that even those entities, noble as they are, might better be part of a ten-way tie for second place. Instead, we should seek the absolutely most noble, incorruptible, and even holy thing for the center of our lives and definition of our identities. When we do that, we can judge our success by the degree to which we have been true to that one thing and to the priorities derived from it. We are called to commitment rather than achievement. Achievement will follow as a byproduct of our faithfulness to our central values, our authentic identity.

We are freed from the hopeless trap of demanding of ourselves perfection and accomplishment measured against a set of standards set by others. We can judge our own success by our commitment and fidelity to our ideals.

We know that this understanding is right. It makes sense down deep. We see it in the people whose stories inspire awe. From it comes the motivation and inspiration to take care of self, family, community, nation, and the world.

You have enjoyed the kind of freedom at Emory to be accepted for who you are. You have demonstrated the freedom to invite others to express their own authentic identity. And that is the lesson that I wanted to remind you about as you leave this place. Keeping the lesson fresh will require that you continue with integrity your homework assignments of reflection, observation, honesty, and devotion. Although there is no assigned reading, wisdom literature is highly recommended. There are no scheduled exams, but there will be frequent popquizzes, perhaps almost daily. I expect you to maintain the high grades that you have earned already.

My prayer for you is that God will bless you bless us—with discernment to know what must be in the center of our lives and the courage to remain committed to it in order authentically to be ourselves. The psalmist said, "Oh Lord, you have sought me and known me." May we always seek to be authentically who we are and who we are called to be.

Part 5

What You Take With You

Growing Wise through Moral Judgment

Two months ago, at a meeting of a small group of students, one of you graduating seniors asked me, "Do you have any concerns for those of us who are graduating?" It was a question I had never been asked before, so my answer was completely off the cuff. "Do I have any concerns for you? Well, one concern I have is that you will forget."

I'm not terribly concerned that you will forget what you learned in the classroom. You will forget a fair measure of that. But at least you will have a document—your transcript—that provides a record of what you have been exposed to and what you once knew. You might even keep a few textbooks and graded essays or exams to refresh those memories from the classroom.

But there will be little record, and certainly no transcript, of the lessons you learned and habits you developed outside the classroom. Perhaps you've never cataloged them in your own mind, and yet they may be some of the most important lessons you've learned. So it may be worth taking a moment to reflect on those. In particular, I want to talk about the lessons you've learned about engagement.

In the Hebrew Bible, we read the great prophet Isaiah reflecting on what he understood to be a holy charge. He proclaims that the spirit of the Lord is upon him, and that he has been anointed to bring good news to the oppressed, to bind up the brokenhearted, to proclaim liberty to those who are captive, to comfort those who mourn. It is a profound call of service to others. It is a call that would not lead him to seek advice from the "self-improvement" section of the Barnes and Noble bookstore. On the contrary, it would lead him to explore the cares and needs of those around him. It's a call to "other improvement," not "self-improvement." But improving the lot of others in a humble rather than patronizing and condescending way. This is a very positive illustration of engagement.

A less positive illustration can be found in a scene from the life of Jesus. He was viewed by many as a great teacher, a rabbi. He was suspected by some to be the Messiah. But in any case, he was understood to be a person of influence and authority. The Gospel of Matthew tells of a time when this authority figure has a crowd of some five thousand gathered around him. He teaches them for a while, and then, suddenly, it's time for a meal. People are hungry. But no one has given any advance thought to feeding such a large group. So with an understandable logic and a sense of expectation, maybe even a sense of entitlement, the disciples advise Jesus that they need to distance themselves from this problem by sending the people away to fend for themselves. Either that or you need to act, Mr. Authority. Do something!

That seems to be the way of the world, or at least the developed world, doesn't it? If there is a problem, "the government" needs to fix it, or "the administration" needs to address it, or "the courts" need to resolve it. But in this case, the authority turns that kind of thinking and expectation back on itself. Jesus turns to those who have brought this community concern forward and says, "You give them something to eat." Don't pass the buck. *You* address it. You own it. You roll up your sleeves. You solve it. And perhaps if you will do that, your efforts will yield miraculous results.

As Emory students, you may find this story unremarkable—this notion that you can make a difference, shape change, help, care, heal, improve, not practice the art of disengagement, of distancing yourselves from each other or from the needs of others. Instead, you have been an engaged society of a sort that can serve elsewhere. If you will not forget.

Let's get specific. Just what have you done that illustrates your engagement with each other, a level of engagement that has become all too uncommon? For one thing, you have shown humanity and sensitivity to the humanity of others. You may have seen those black-and-white TV commercials that have become popular. They are not entirely black and white. Rather, the scene and the people are rendered in black and white, but the product being sold, to which your eye is drawn, is in full color. It's a very effective way to narrow the focus of the viewer.

But sometimes we view our world, and especially other people, the same way. Most of the world is monochrome. Most of the people in the world, in our city, in our community, in our neighborhood or apartment building are black and white. They are animate cogs in the machinery of community. Only that inner circle of family and friends do we render in full, living color. We only know well a small coterie with whom we are certain that we will feel comfortable.

In our companies and institutions—even Emory—we use terms like "human resources." Have you ever thought about how dehumanizing that term is? The word "human" is reduced to an adjective describing a form of resource.

But you have not (yet) come to view the human family as human resources rendered in black and white. You threw yourselves open to show your colors to others. You have cared about the subtle hues in each other. I know that, because you have done so even in your dealings with me. In my weekly student office hours and in e-mails from you, I find it remarkable how often you have asked how I am doing—and have actually meant it. "We heard that your father died. How are you doing?" "Your wife tells us that your daughter will be married this summer. How is that coming? How are you doing?" "This labor matter is a difficult one for you, I can tell. How are you doing?" All of that is just to me, the president, about whom you could be completely forgiven for caring very little except about what money I might be able to allocate to your club or what authority I might be able to exercise in your behalf. Your genuine recognition of me in full color has touched me. I hope you always will bring such attention to those whom you treat as people instead of human resources or human cogs.

But this will take work—hard work to remember and continue to apply this lesson. Many of you will enter communities where the norm is not only to neglect the colors in each other but to avert your eyes altogether, to avoid interaction on the sidewalk. Many will encounter that pervasive myth that while there is certainly great opportunity or great need, the burden is far too great for you to become engaged. But you know better. You know that it is possible to own and be proud of a community, a city, a state, a nation, a world, even as you have been proud of Emory, warts and all. By remaining engaged with each other's humanity, we discover more moments of celebration and more opportunities for service, both hallmarks of Emory community.

Another example of how you have grown wise in the ways of engagement is your evident lack of fear in exercising judgment in your own behalf and that of others. We live in a culture uncomfortable with the exercise of judgment, not in the sense of passing judgment but in the sense of exercising wisdom. We prefer to form opinions and make decisions based on fact sheets and spreadsheets. But data sets don't cooperate as we would like. If they did, we could employ computers instead of teachers, advisers, physicians, legislators, and parents. Not all decisions can be arrived at with integrity unless we exercise thoughtful reflection and consideration over sparse data and principle.

We often don't like to stick our necks out to exercise judgment and don't like it when others do. We tell our teachers to teach to the test rather than exercise judgment about what each individual student needs. We elect representatives to positions in government and tell them to exercise their judgment but then are appalled when their decisions do not map onto opinion polls. Though having said that, I am glad—and am sure that you are—that in 1964, Congress approved the Civil Rights Act when opinion polls would have instructed them to do otherwise. Polls will give us comforting numbers about like-minded persons, but they defeat the exercise of judgment.

Judgment of course requires some facility with facts, but it also requires an understanding of moral principle. That in turn takes energy—the energy to open ourselves and to engage meaningfully with each other about ideas and views. This is the hard work of engagement.

You have exercised a remarkable openness to opinions and perspectives from many sides. Incorporating those ideas with the facts and moral principle, you have proven adept at exercising judgment. You have contributed to the notion that the word "liberal" needs to be understood as the opposite of "illiberal." That a truly liberal community invites and considers conservative views with the same curiosity and potential for legitimacy as it welcomes progressive views. It is no secret that, when you leave our community, the word "liberal" will be used more often than not as a label and not a description of a practice of good judgment.

Other lessons of engagement that you have learned include genuine communication, authenticity, community service, and your responsibility to make diversity more than politically correct tolerance. But more of these practices of engagement derive from your commitment to take one another seriously, to see and be seen in full color, and to exercise the discipline of good judgment, deciding for yourselves rather than going with the flow of someone else's judgment.

"You give them something to eat," Jesus said. You do it. Take with you that community ethic that you so well developed here. There is a hunger for real people to return and build integrity into our community life, just as you have done here. You would not have gotten up early to be part of this service this morning if you did not imagine that there is something worth celebrating about the community that you have built. Perhaps for some of you, there is even a sense of sadness to be leaving all that is good here. If that is the case, then don't leave it. Take it with you. Apply these lessons in whatever community you find yourself in in the future. "You do it," he said—and expect miracles of the transformative kind that you have worked during your time here.

More Worthy Aspiration

Class of 2007, you are the first class at Emory with whom I have spent an entire four years, so I confess that I have a particular affection for this class. In fact, because of that affection, I am tempted to act as your parents might have acted four years ago. You know—"There's just one more thing I'd like to tell you before you go."

So let me reflect with you a little about "aspiration." It's not that you need more of it! Students have no lack of things to aspire to. But the nature of your aspirations as you leave here should be different from those you brought with you. You came with great aspirations, certainly, but I suggest that they may have been motivated principally by ambition, somewhat unfocused, and in fact maybe not even your own so much as those of your parents, families, or peers.

So what makes aspiration worthy and noble rather than small and misdirected?

The Christian scriptures tell the story of the mother of two young men, James and John. She approaches Jesus and asks, "Grant that one of these two sons of mine may sit at your right and the other at your left when you come into your kingdom." This story takes place in first-century, Roman-occupied Judaea. James and John are brothers who have been part of a small group of followers of Jesus during his ministry. They are coming to imagine that he may be the long-prophesied Messiah of the Jews, although later events will show that they really do not know exactly what that means. But Mom thinks that she knows. Just in case this Jesus turns out to be the next king who will restore the sovereignty of Israel, she wants to be sure that her boys are not left out of the royal court. So she demands, "When this all works out, commit to me that my boys will be your chief cabinet officers—your right- and left-hand men."

There is so much wrong about this request. Take the object of the aspiration. Clearly, it is personal glorification—elevation to a position of honor. But the aspiration to be great, revered, honored is simply naked ambition, not aspiration. Ambition is selfish aspiration.

The rebuke that the mother of James and John receives for her request makes it clear that wise aspiration does not seek self-promotion and is not motivated by ambition. Rather, its aim is service. Jesus tells James and John, "Whoever wants to become great among you must be your servant, and whoever wants to be first must be your slave."

This is wise advice. But understandably, it sinks into most of us late in life. When we are children, we are the centers of our own universe, and we believe that we are the center of our parents' universe as well. Naturally, we assign our highest aspirations to the most important things in our universe—us! But life in general, and university education in particular, teaches us a way of viewing the world from others' perspectives.

Not long ago, I was watching a recorded lecture by our own professor of history Patrick Allitt. He was speaking about Andrew Carnegie, a steel magnate at the beginning of the twentieth century, who later became a leading philanthropist. Among his philanthropic aspirations was the wish to give opportunity to the poor. But he opposed simply giving them money on the principle that doing so would produce dependency, not inspire effort or aspiration. So he used a portion of his philanthropic largess to establish public libraries—more than twenty-seven hundred of them, as I recall.

Carnegie also hated class systems, so he opposed the practice of inheritance. Instead of passing large fortunes along to one's children, Carnegie advocated leaving one's wealth for uses beyond the family. The extraordinary American tradition of philanthropy owes a great deal to the example of Andrew Carnegie.

From this description of Carnegie's later life, he sounds like a wise and generous person, and indeed he appears to have become that. But in his early years, while making all of that money, he exercised ruthlessness in enforcing long hours and paying low wages in harsh steel-mill environments. He was similarly ruthless and violent in squashing labor organization. Only late in his life did he develop or respond to this impulse to philanthropic aspirations.

Carnegie's story of transformation from ambition to aspiration is not uncommon. Other robber barons of his age included men whose names we all recognize, like tobacco giant James Buchannan Duke, oil monopolist John D. Rockefeller, and shipping magnate Cornelius Vanderbilt—all of whom, as Professor Allitt notes, "sterilized" their nasty reputations by establishing foundations and universities late in their lives. We can be happy for those philanthropic legacies, but not necessarily happy for what Carnegie called the "uneasy conscience" that these men suffered prior to reassessing their aspirations. It makes one wonder if there would be much overlap between the list of the world's hundred wealthiest people and the world's hundred happiest people.

About this notion of aspiration, then, we can learn from James and John, and from Carnegie, Vanderbilt, Duke, and Rockefeller. Do we wish to follow their pattern of being great and then good, or do we believe that it is possible to go through life seeking to be both good *and* great? As a first step, we can ask ourselves about the objects of our aspirations.

- Do I want to be a music star or to compose and perform the world's best music?
- Do I want to be a noted physician or to contribute powerfully to health and healing?
- Do I wish to be a wealthy businessman or a principled leader for global enterprise?
- Do I wish to be a highly respected attorney or to work for justice?
- Do I wish to be a tenured professor at a distinguished university or a passionate scholar and teacher?
- Do I aspire for self-advancement or to a purpose much larger than me?

If the object of our aspirations is worth asking questions about, so is the ownership of our aspirations. Who really owns our aspirations?

Today is Mother's Day, and we honor our mothers for their love and their commitment to our meaningful success. But this request by the mother of James and John is an example of helicopter parenting of the highest degree—millennia before helicopters were invented!

The message is clear: as we mature, *we* are to become the principal owners of our aspirations. Yet we should not be deaf to those whose wisdom and love for us can offer guidance. We should seek mentoring from those we admire and guidance from what we hold as holy. But in the final analysis, *we* must own our aspirations—not our families, not the pressures and expectations of our friends, not the messages of popular culture, and not even the stale promises that we made to ourselves long ago. Joseph Campbell said that we must be open to letting go of the life we had planned in order to be open to the life that awaits us.

That brings us to a question about the source of our aspirations. Where do our aspirations come from?

There is another story to consider. It is the story of the calling of the prophet Samuel in the Hebrew Bible. As a young boy, Samuel has been placed in the temple to care for the aging priest Eli. One night, Samuel is aroused from his sleep when he hears his name called. Assuming that Eli is calling, he checks in with the fatherly priest. But Eli has not called Samuel and sends him back to bed. This calling and response repeats itself three times before Eli suggests that the call is coming from the Lord. Eli instructs young Samuel that if the call comes again, he should acknowledge it and listen.

We use the word "call" infrequently, but it is actually a very common phenomenon—that feeling that we are being impelled toward a certain course of action. We feel it often. Far less common is our willingness to listen and to discern its meaning. We are fond of fatalistic aphorisms suggesting that we are the product of our DNA or our upbringing as though our lives are ultimately determined by childhood or by our biology. Sometimes life would be easier if that were true. From time to time, I will ask a student about career aspirations. Often I'll hear something like, "Everyone in my family is a physician, so I guess I will be too." As I said, there is a certain comfort in that. It is easier than trying to be attentive to a call and to one's own aspiration.

But we should not ignore those calls in the still, small hours of the night. We should listen, be open, and respond.

Unfortunately, listening has become more difficult. Radio, television, and iPods have turned us into listeners with too much power. We have full control of the volume and of the select and pause buttons. We listen when we want to listen and only to what we want to hear. Even in conversation, listening has become something of a lost art. Eager to make our points in a conversation, we reduce listening to the period of downtime between our opportunities to speak. But listening is work—whether having the patience to hear others out or committing contemplatively to discern a call.

Where does a call itself come from? From everywhere—from parents, friends, wise elders, professors, inspiring lives, and, as in Samuel's case, from God. In fact, it is from these same places that we receive help in examining the merits of the calls that we hear.

Four years ago, while most of you were heeding a call to come to Emory, I was resisting the call to be considered for Emory's presidency. It was not that there was anything wrong with Emory; it was just that the timing was very bad. Our family was settled in Cleveland, our younger daughter was a rising senior in high school, and Case Western Reserve University had just hired a president with whom I was enjoying the challenge of helping to move his ideas toward success. When I pointed out to a wise mentor the difficulties of the timing, he remarked, "Bad things in your life never happen when you want them to. Then why do you think that good things should?" Like Samuel, I was being told to go and listen and to discern whether there was a call to be attended to.

Finally, we should consider the temporal qualities of our aspirations. Time horizons change throughout our lives, most dramatically during our college years. Try to recall how far away this graduation week felt when you entered Emory as freshmen. With an appreciation for the speed of passing time, we should consider just how far into the future to place the objects of our aspirations. Not all of us here today need to be clear about our aspirations regarding retirement. But long-term aspirations challenge us. They give us a sense of purpose and drive.

Still, there are dangers in setting long-term goals. We can become doggedly committed to a specific and narrowly defined aspiration. This can lead to disappointment when life circumstances conspire to defeat our plans. Blind doggedness also can deafen us to midlife callings that might take us in new directions more marvelously rewarding and satisfying than our initial goals. And, most insidious, there is the danger that we will cling so rigidly to our aspirations that we will not allow ourselves to enjoy the present.

The sure marks of a true and noble aspiration are the enthusiasm and genuine joy it ignites in the present. This kind of joy has less to do with happiness and more to do with hope and confidence. The happiness born of a noble aspiration, even in the midst of difficult circumstances and hard work, is as satisfying as any expectation of reward. Said another way, living miserable lives for the sake of joyless aspirations should prompt us to reevaluate those aspirations. Pursuit of noble aspirations and true calling are continuing sources of joy.

So my wish for you is that you will be deliberate about setting the aspirations that guide you—their purpose, their authenticity as truly yours, their source of inspiration and calling, and the present joy that they bring.

May God bless you with

clear and noble aspirations to give you purpose;
ownership of your aspirations to give you a sense of identity;
rich faith and confidence in the source of your aspirations; and
joy in the daily pursuit of your dreams.

HUMILITY AS VIRTUE, NOT AFFLICTION

Consider the lowly term humility. It sounds a bit dull, not all that interesting. In part, this is because the concept has drifted far from its virtuous roots.

When we think of humility, we might imagine Winnie-the-Pooh's friend Eeyore, the donkey. Poor Eeyore had such low self-esteem that he thanked people just for noticing him! That kind of humility, derived from frailty, weakness, and a low sense of self-worth, isn't very attractive. Nor is it all that virtuous. It neither lifts the individual up nor provides a platform from which to serve society. Instead, it can be paralyzing and depressing, inhibiting the joy of risk-taking and the satisfaction of meeting challenges of life.

I want to try to reaffirm humility as a virtue rather than an affliction. For something to be virtuous, it must have intrinsic value—value to the individual and to the broader community; something worthy of respect, appreciation, and admiration. Self-diminishing humility is, by definition, of low value, not a virtue.

In the Hebrew Bible, the prophet Micah helps us to understand the notion of value and maybe, thereby, the notion of virtue. Micah is one of the so-called minor prophets of the Abrahamic faiths of Judaism, Christianity, and Islam. In one well-known passage, he attempts to answer the questions, just what is it that God wants of us? What is really of value in life? What is most important?

Micah responds to these questions by listing all the possible personal sacrifices that sound most impressive and virtuous. In the market language of his time, he lists burnt offerings of thousands of rams and ten thousand rivers of oil. Even the dedication of one's firstborn child to God's service instead of the family business.

But Micah soon recognizes that giving away material goods, even to religious institutions, is not the point of a life well lived. Commercial profits, inflation-proof acquisitions, even one's firstborn child—none of these rank among the most valuable of ultimate gifts. So what are we living for? What are we working for? Why did you struggle for the best grades possible if they are not the most valuable fruits of your life?

The fact is that Micah never says that any of those things lack value. He does not denigrate hard work or the love of parents for their children or even the practice of sacrifice. But Micah is saying that there is something even more important than giving to worthy causes—something more important than our symbolic and most genuinely pious practices. Micah lays it out clearly:

> The Lord has shown you, O mortal, what is good.
> And what does the LORD require of you?
> To act justly and to love mercy
> and to walk humbly with your God.

What matters is not what we do with what we possess and control. More important is how we go about the business of this experience called life. It is fine to amass wealth and achieve success. More important is how we do that. Will we do it with the false belief that those are the most valuable things in life, so that any means to acquire them is justified? Or will we recognize that material ends are secondary to justice, kindness, and humility?

Those virtues of justice and kindness are certainly worth examining. But I am impressed and a bit surprised by what Micah implies about real humility. The humility spoken about in this passage is not what typically comes to mind when we hear the word. Instead of being a habit of self-effacement, it is a choice, something taken on because it has immense intrinsic value, leading to a way of life that is uplifting.

Consider the suggestion that humility can be positively chosen. In the passage I've quoted, the virtues of justice and kindness and humility are referred to as requirements. "What does the Lord *require* of you?" Just as there is no such thing as passive kindness or passive justice, so the kind of humility spoken of here must be active, striding out, exercised all along our way.

But if humility is an active virtue rather than simply characteristic of an unimposing life or the byproduct of low self-esteem, how do we practice it deliberately, beyond just avoiding pride and arrogance? In a nutshell, we do it by seeking out circumstances that place us in a subordinate status. We practice it by looking for and placing ourselves deliberately in humbling circumstances.

Now this is not as bad as it might sound. When we pursue this sort of humility, we find ourselves at the base of tall mountains or in view of beautiful sunsets; we find ourselves in the presence of men and women of superior intellect, experience, talent, and character. In fact, this sort of humility begins to sound appealing. Still, it does not necessarily come naturally; it can be uncomfortable. But it can yield great satisfaction of service, personal growth, and even thrills. Yes, thrills—about which, more later.

So humility can be pursued deliberately, but what about the claim that it has extraordinary value? The entire passage in Micah is about values and valuables—calves, rams, precious oil, yes—but also justice, kindness, and humility. All are listed nearly within a single breath. Humility is among the valuables. Note also that the passage imagines that those who walk humbly are in a position to offer justice and kindness. They will have substantial worth to others. No room for low self-esteem here.

Actually, you have practiced intentional humility with some regularity on this campus during your years at Emory. You may not always have recognized what you were doing as practicing humility. Where have you practiced intentional and edifying humility? Where have you willingly sought out and placed yourself in circumstances where you were not the best, most experienced, widely read, or best prepared? At the very least, that has happened in the classroom, again and again, in the presence of your professors.

So you have made an excellent start. You have experienced the value of placing yourself in humbling circumstances. And the value of those experiences, the riches of such humility, is inestimable.

That kind of deliberate seeking of humbling opportunities is the basis for some of the most satisfying moments in life. To fully know the thrill of risk-taking in business, personal relationships, sports, leadership, creativity, and service requires the pursuit and exercise of humility. Take any example. Learning to hit a softball or play on a team entails submitting to something well beyond our natural inclinations. Committing to marriage or starting a new business requires the courage to recognize your discomfort, to test your ability, to be uncertain about your worth in such circumstances, and yet to go forward anyhow. From such can come thrilling achievement.

Then there are the thrills of service. You know about those thrills also. In the spring of your junior year, *USA TODAY* published the results of a poll indicating that 59 percent of American undergraduate students claim to have participated meaningfully in a service-learning program or in service outreach. That is an encouraging number. But Emory students reported an 87 percent rate. You know something about service and its satisfactions. Were you not in awe of the need when you volunteered in New Orleans, visited Africa, served at Grady Hospital, participated in Volunteer Emory, or simply comforted a crying friend? You were in awe *not* because your circumstances and abilities were superior to someone else's, but because the circumstances gave you something accessible only through the act of your humble attempt to assist. Quieting your ego and ignoring your dignity enough to actually see the circumstances of others and then finding deep meaning in serving them is a clear reward from this active form of humility.

Finally, there is the humility that allows us to enjoy the awesome qualities of inspiring individuals, natural and artistically created beauty, or the presence of the wonderful and the holy. This thrill is completely inaccessible to us without courageous practice. Responding to the command to walk humbly with our God, and by extension to walk with and be in the presence of what is great and holy—this is not a sacrifice but instead a privilege. Many of you have had opportunities to be in the presence of greatness, or at least in the presence of those who have great achievements to their name. Maybe you met or dined with Salman Rushdie or received a greeting from the Dalai Lama. Those occasions,

I'm sure, were thrilling and edifying. And you did not need to focus on quieting your ego to act humbly. Instead, humility came naturally in those circumstances.

True humility, then, is not about lowering ourselves but about recognizing what elevates us in those circumstances when we are, in fact, inferior, humble. There are only two tricks for receiving the gifts of this virtue. The first is actively to seek the things that inspire awe—friends, family, literature, art, science, commerce, and service. And the second is to be aware and awake, not failing to notice what inspires and humbles us every day, and helping others to be aware of it as well.

Your experiences while at Emory have given you sharper sight and more acute ears. You possess more knowledge and power of interpretation than you have ever had before and that relatively few in the entire world ever will have. You could be proud of your extraordinary capacity and seek personal gain through position and vanity. Or you can have more. You can use your gifts and powers humbly to pursue what is both great and good, both for your own deep joy and for the deep joy of others.

May God grant you

> the determination, wisdom, and humility to seek and experience awe;
> the courage to use your great capacities for genuine humility; and
> the joy of walking humbly in the presence of the great and the holy.